USBORNE SPOTTER'S GUIDES

Flags of the World

Phil Clarke

Designed by Michael Hill
Flag consultant: Jos Poel

Introduction

This book will help you identify the flags of every independent country in the world, and several territories (places governed by others). The entries are ordered by geography with **key facts** below. There is an alphabetical **index** at the back, as well as a list of in-depth **features** that will tell you more about the history and influence of famous flags.

Each entry is laid out like this:

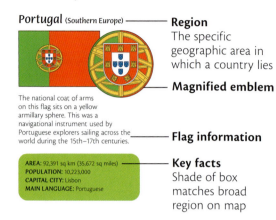

- North America 4-11
- South America 12-14
- Europe 15-27
- Africa 28-41
- Asia 42-56
- Oceania 57-61

Emblems

Some flags feature an **emblem**. It may be a coat of arms or other symbol important to the nation. Some varieties of emblem are shown on the right.

National symbols
(Canada)

Natural features
(Kiribati)

Coats of arms
(Mexico)

Religious symbols: *above* Georgia's Christian crosses; *below* the Islamic star and crescent of Pakistan

Flags with an emblem or script are made so that the emblem faces the same way on both sides.

Parts of a flag

Flags are usually made of cloth. One edge is folded into a tube called the **sleeve**. The half of the flag nearest the sleeve is called the **hoist**. The half that flaps in the wind is the **fly**. The upper part of the hoist is the **canton**.

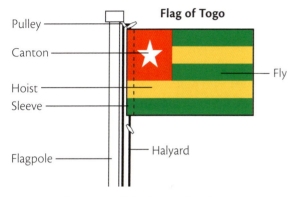

To raise a flag, you pull the **halyard** and fasten it at the bottom of the **flagpole**.

All flags have a front, called the **obverse**, and a back, the **reverse**. The obverse is the side you see when the pole is on the left. The reverse of the flag is usually a mirror image of the obverse.

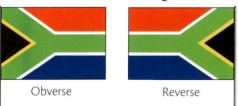

Spotting flags

Once you start looking, you'll spot flags everywhere: on the news; at international sporting events or song contests; and flying outside government buildings, embassies or big hotels.

The designs of some flags are so famous that you'll even see them used on clothing and bags.

Flag design

As you spot flags, you'll see that they fall into groups with similar designs.

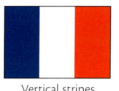

Vertical stripes (France)

Horizontal stripes (Sierra Leone)

Stripes with emblem (Ghana)

Stripes with emblem in canton (Malaysia)

Nordic cross (Finland)

Triangle (Bahamas)

Usborne Quicklinks

For links to websites where you can find out more about flags, go to **usborne.com/Quicklinks** and enter the keywords: **world flags** Usborne Publishing is not responsible for the content or availability of external websites.

3

United States (North America)

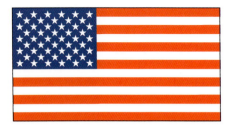

The 50 stars represent the US states, and the 13 stripes stand for the original colonies that won their independence from Britain in 1776.
Nicknames: Stars and Stripes, Star-Spangled Banner, Old Glory
Similar: Liberia (31), Malaysia (54)

AREA: 9,522,055 sq km (3,676,486 sq miles)
POPULATION: 341,814,000
CAPITAL CITY: Washington, DC
MAIN LANGUAGE: English

Canada (North America)

Canada is famous for its maple trees. The maple leaf on its flag is its national symbol. The white square between two red bands is said to symbolize Canada's place between the Pacific and Atlantic Oceans.
Nicknames: The Maple Leaf; *l'Unifolié* (French for *the single-leaved*)

AREA: 9,984,670 sq km (3,855,103 sq miles)
POPULATION: 39,107,000
CAPITAL CITY: Ottawa
MAIN LANGUAGES: English, French

History of the Stars and Stripes

In 1776, American soldiers fought under the Grand Union flag (below left) as they battled for independence from Britain. This flag, inspired by the red-and-white striped flags of American merchant ships, became the first flag of the USA. Since then, it has been updated 26 times. First, the British flag in the corner was replaced with 13 stars for the 13 colonies. Then in 1818, a new law decreed that the flag would gain a star for every state to join the Union – even today, their number could grow.

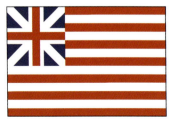

Grand Union flag

Betsy Ross flag, an early design

Greenland (North America)

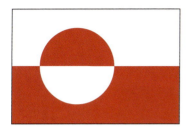

Greenland is part of the Kingdom of Denmark, its flag reflecting the red and white of the Danish flag (17). It is known as *Erfalasorput* (our flag) or *Aappalaartoq* (the red) in Greenlandic. It symbolizes the ice of this large island nation and the sun setting over the sea.

AREA: 2,166,086 sq km (836,330 sq miles)
POPULATION: 57,000
CAPITAL CITY: Nuuk
MAIN LANGUAGES: Greenlandic, Danish

Bermuda (North America)

Bermuda is a British Overseas Territory. Its flag is the Red Ensign of the UK Merchant Navy with Bermuda's coat of arms. This is a red lion holding a shield depicting the wreck of the ship *Sea Venture*, which was driven to the then-uninhabited islands by a hurricane in 1609.

AREA: 53 sq km (20 sq miles)
POPULATION: 64,000
CAPITAL CITY: Hamilton
MAIN LANGUAGES: Bermudian English, Portuguese

Mexico (North America)

The emblem on this flag shows the legend of the founding of Mexico City. Ancient Mexicans, called Aztecs, saw a golden eagle eating a snake on a prickly pear cactus, on an island in a lake. They took it as an omen that their capital city should be built there. **Similar:** Italy (21)

AREA: 1,972,550 sq km (761,606 sq miles)
POPULATION: 129,388,000
CAPITAL CITY: Mexico City
MAIN LANGUAGES: Spanish, Nahuatl, Mayan

Belize (Central America)

Belize used to be a UK colony, British Honduras. Its flag shows its old coat of arms, which features symbols of its history in the mahogany timber trade. The motto is *Sub umbra floreo*, Latin for *I flourish in the shade*.

AREA: 22,966 sq km (8,867 sq miles)
POPULATION: 417,000
CAPITAL CITY: Belmopan
MAIN LANGUAGES: English, Creole, Spanish, Mayan

Guatemala (Central America)

The coat of arms includes a laurel wreath, symbolizing victory. In the middle is a scroll with Guatemala's date of independence from Spain: September 15, 1821. Perched on top is a green quetzal bird, a national symbol of freedom.

AREA: 108,890 sq km (42,042 sq miles)
POPULATION: 18,358,000
CAPITAL CITY: Guatemala City
MAIN LANGUAGES: Spanish, Mayan languages

El Salvador (Central America)

From 1823–1841, El Salvador and four other Central American nations (see Honduras) were part of a big country called the Federal Republic of Central America. Its flag inspired El Salvador's. The white and blue bands represent the land of Central America, lying between two oceans. **Similar:** Nicaragua

AREA: 21,040 sq km (8,124 sq miles)
POPULATION: 6,396,000
CAPITAL CITY: San Salvador
MAIN LANGUAGE: Spanish

Honduras (Central America)

Five countries once made up a larger nation named the Federal Republic of Central America. Along with Honduras were Guatemala, El Salvador, Nicaragua and Costa Rica. The five stars on the Honduran flag recall that unity.

AREA: 112,090 sq km (43,278 sq miles)
POPULATION: 10,759,000
CAPITAL CITY: Tegucigalpa
MAIN LANGUAGE: Spanish

Nicaragua (Central America)

In the middle of this flag is the country's full name encircling its coat of arms. The triangular emblem features five volcanoes, symbolizing five countries that once formed the Federal Republic of Central America. **Similar:** Argentina (14)

AREA: 129,494 sq km (49,998 sq miles)
POPULATION: 7,143,000
CAPITAL CITY: Managua
MAIN LANGUAGE: Spanish

Costa Rica (Central America)

The red band added to the traditional Central American blue and white stripes (see El Salvador) was inspired by the French flag (18), whose stripes represent liberty, equality and togetherness. **Similar:** Thailand (54)

AREA: 51,100 sq km (19,730 sq miles)
POPULATION: 5,247,000
CAPITAL CITY: San José
MAIN LANGUAGE: Spanish

Panama (Central America)

Red and blue stand for two rival political parties. The white stands for the peace that brought them together to found a new nation in 1903, when Panama became independent from Colombia. Many merchant ships are registered in Panama, and they fly its flag.

AREA: 78,200 sq km (30,193 sq miles)
POPULATION: 4,528,000
CAPITAL CITY: Panama City
MAIN LANGUAGE: Spanish

Bahamas (Caribbean)

The black triangle on this flag symbolizes the power and purpose of the Bahamian people as they join together. The yellow stripe represents the rich resources of their land, the aquamarine (greenish-blue) stripes, those of the sea around them.

AREA: 13,940 sq km (5,382 sq miles)
POPULATION: 415,000
CAPITAL CITY: Nassau
MAIN LANGUAGES: Bahamian Creole, English

Cuba (Caribbean)

This flag was inspired by the US flag (4). The three blue stripes stand for the regions of Cuba. The triangle represents liberty, equality and togetherness. The white star originally signified Cuba's desire to become a US state. For Cubans today, it is a symbol of freedom.

AREA: 110,860 sq km (42,803 sq miles)
POPULATION: 11,175,000
CAPITAL CITY: Havana
MAIN LANGUAGE: Spanish

Cayman Islands (Caribbean)

The flag of the Cayman Islands, a British Overseas Territory, is the UK Blue Ensign (see 57) with their coat of arms. The turtle above recalls the Spanish name *Las Tortugas* (The Turtles) given to the islands by the explorer Christopher Columbus, after the many he saw there.

AREA: 259 sq km (100 sq miles)
POPULATION: 70,000
CAPITAL CITY: George Town
MAIN LANGUAGE: English

Jamaica (Caribbean)

Jamaica's is the only national flag that contains no red, white or blue. It first flew in 1962, when Jamaica became independent from Britain. Its meaning has been explained in the saying: *Hardships there are* (black), *but the land is green and the sun still shines* (yellow).

AREA: 10,991 sq km (4,244 sq miles)
POPULATION: 2,825,000
CAPITAL CITY: Kingston
MAIN LANGUAGES: Caribbean Creole, English

Haiti (Caribbean)

In 1803, Haitian rebels tore the white stripe from the flag of their French rulers (18) and made a new blue and red one from the remains. They added a coat of arms, which features a red cap as a symbol of revolution.
Similar: Liechtenstein (20)

AREA: 27,750 sq km (10,714 sq miles)
POPULATION: 11,867,000
CAPITAL CITY: Port-au-Prince
MAIN LANGUAGES: Haitian Creole, French

Dominican Republic (Caribbean)

In 1844, the Dominican Republic won independence from Haiti, and hoisted Haiti's flag with a white cross added to symbolize the Catholic faith. Later, the red and blue rectangles on the fly edge were swapped over.

AREA: 48,380 sq km (18,815 sq miles)
POPULATION: 11,434,000
CAPITAL CITY: Santo Domingo
MAIN LANGUAGE: Spanish

Puerto Rico (Caribbean)

The flag of Puerto Rico, a US territory since 1898, was inspired by those of Cuba (7) and the USA (4). It was recognized as the official standard of Puerto Rico in 1952, when the island nation became a self-governing US Commonwealth.

AREA: 9,104 sq km (3,515 sq miles)
POPULATION: 3,269,000
CAPITAL CITY: San Juan
MAIN LANGUAGES: Spanish, English

British Virgin Islands (Caribbean)

The coat of arms on the flag of this British Overseas Territory shows Saint Ursula, the virgin princess for whom Columbus named the islands. The 11 oil lamps stand for Ursula's 11,000 virgin companions, who legend says were all killed with her on pilgrimage.

AREA: 153 sq km (59 sq miles)
POPULATION: 32,000
CAPITAL CITY: Road Town
MAIN LANGUAGES: English, Caribbean Creole

US Virgin Islands (Caribbean)

St Croix, St Thomas and St John are the three biggest of those Virgin Islands that belong to the United States. They are represented on this flag by three arrows in the claw of the American eagle. This flag was first used in 1921.

AREA: 356 sq km (134 sq miles)
POPULATION: 98,000
CAPITAL CITY: Charlotte Amalie
MAIN LANGUAGES: English, Spanish

St Kitts and Nevis (Caribbean)

The black stripe symbolizes the African roots of most of the people of St Kitts and Nevis (St Kitts is short for St Christopher). The stars represent the two islands, and also hope and freedom. The green stands for fertile land, the red for the struggle to be free, and the yellow for sunshine.

AREA: 261 sq km (101 sq miles)
POPULATION: 48,000
CAPITAL CITY: Basseterre
MAIN LANGUAGES: English, Caribbean Creole

Antigua and Barbuda (Caribbean)

The rising sun symbolizes these islands' new start as a self-ruling state in 1967. Red stands for a dynamic people, and black for their African heritage. Yellow, blue and white are for sun, sea and sand. The "V" shape is for victory.

AREA: 443 sq km (171 sq miles)
POPULATION: 95,000
CAPITAL CITY: St John's
MAIN LANGUAGES: Caribbean Creole, English

Dominica (Caribbean)

Dominica's flag features its national bird, the endangered Sisserou parrot. Green represents the island's lush forests; the red circle, a fair society; and the triple cross, Christianity. Yellow stands for citrus, bananas, and native peoples; black for soil and Africa; white for clear rivers and purity.

AREA: 754 sq km (291 sq miles)
POPULATION: 73,000
CAPITAL CITY: Roseau
MAIN LANGUAGES: English, Antillean Creole

St Lucia (Caribbean)

The triangles depict the Pitons, St Lucia's twin peaks of volcanic rock. Black and white symbolize different races living in peace. Yellow stands for sunshine, and blue for the Caribbean Sea and Atlantic Ocean.

AREA: 616 sq km (239 sq miles)
POPULATION: 181,000
CAPITAL CITY: Castries
MAIN LANGUAGES: English, Antillean Creole

St Vincent and the Grenadines (Caribbean)

St Vincent and the 32 Grenadines are known as *the Gems of the Antilles*. The Antilles is the great chain of islands that borders the Caribbean. The green gems are arranged in a "V" for St Vincent.

AREA: 389 sq km (150 sq miles)
POPULATION: 104,000
CAPITAL CITY: Kingstown
MAIN LANGUAGES: English, Antillean Creole

Barbados (Caribbean)

Until 1966, Barbados was ruled by Britain. Its flag showed Lady Britannia, a symbol of Britain, holding a three-pronged trident. The broken-off top of the trident on the new flag declared Barbados's break from British rule.

AREA: 431 sq km (166 sq miles)
POPULATION: 282,000
CAPITAL CITY: Bridgetown
MAIN LANGUAGES: Caribbean Creole, English

Grenada (Caribbean)

The shape that looks like a flame is actually a nutmeg fruit. The spice, Grenada's main crop, is made from its seed. The flag's outer stars stand for the island's six parishes, and the middle one represents St George's, the capital city.

AREA: 344 sq km (133 sq miles)
POPULATION: 127,000
CAPITAL CITY: St George's
MAIN LANGUAGES: English, Antillean Creole

Trinidad and Tobago (Caribbean)

This flag was first raised when Trinidad and Tobago won independence from British rule in 1962. The two white stripes represent the sea, the red symbolizes the people, and the black signifies their hard work and strength.

AREA: 5,128 sq km (1,980 sq miles)
POPULATION: 1,538,000
CAPITAL CITY: Port of Spain
MAIN LANGUAGES: Caribbean Creole, English

Aruba (Caribbean)

The island country of Aruba belongs to the Kingdom of the Netherlands. It first flew this flag in 1976. The light blue represents the United Nations (see 63) and the sea. The star has four points like a compass, and is red like Aruba's soil. The yellow stripes stand for tourism and industry.

AREA: 180 sq km (70 sq miles)
POPULATION: 106,000
CAPITAL CITY: Oranjestad
MAIN LANGUAGES: Papiamento, Dutch

Colombia (South America)

A Colombian children's song about the flag goes: *Yellow is our gold, blue our vast seas, and red the blood that gave us our freedom.* The design was inspired by the flag of Gran Colombia, a country that once included Colombia, Venezuela and Ecuador.

AREA: 1,138,910 sq km (439,736 sq miles)
POPULATION: 52,341,000
CAPITAL CITY: Bogotá
MAIN LANGUAGE: Spanish

Venezuela (South America)

Yellow stands for the land's wealth, blue for courage, and red for independence. The eight stars symbolize Venezuela's eight regions. The flag is based on one designed in 1811 by Francisco de Miranda, a Venezuelan war hero.

AREA: 912,050 sq km (352,144 sq miles)
POPULATION: 29,395,000
CAPITAL CITY: Caracas
MAIN LANGUAGE: Spanish

Guyana (South America)

Known as the *Golden Arrowhead*, this flag was created for a competition when Guyana became independent from Britain in 1966. Green stands for the rainforest that covers most of Guyana, red for the sacrifice of building a nation, and the arrowhead for the hope of a golden future.

AREA: 214,970 sq km (83,000 sq miles)
POPULATION: 820,000
CAPITAL CITY: Georgetown
MAIN LANGUAGES: Guyanese Creole, English

Suriname (South America)

The flag was first used in 1975, when Suriname became independent from the Netherlands. The stripes represent progress and love (red), hope and fertility (green), and peace, freedom and justice (white). The star symbolizes unity.

AREA: 163,270 sq km (63,039 sq miles)
POPULATION: 629,000
CAPITAL CITY: Paramaribo
MAIN LANGUAGES: Sranan Tongo, Dutch

Ecuador (South America)

The coat of arms features the Guayas River flowing from Mount Chimborazo, Ecuador's highest peak, and a steamboat. A condor, the national bird of Ecuador, protects the nation under its wings. **Similar:** Colombia

> **AREA:** 283,560 sq km (109,483 sq miles)
> **POPULATION:** 18,377,000
> **CAPITAL CITY:** Quito
> **MAIN LANGUAGES:** Spanish, Quechua

Brazil (South America)

The blue circle represents the night sky. Brazil's 27 states are represented by the stars that were over Rio de Janeiro on November 15, 1889, when Brazil became a republic. The banner bears Brazil's motto, *Order and progress*, in Portuguese.

> **AREA:** 8,511,965 sq km (3,286,488 sq miles)
> **POPULATION:** 217,637,000
> **CAPITAL CITY:** Brasília
> **MAIN LANGUAGE:** Portuguese

Peru (South America)

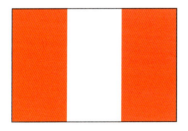

General José de San Martin, who helped to free Peru from Spanish rule, designed its first flag in 1821. His choice of red and white, still in today's flag, is said to have been inspired by the bright red wings and pale bodies of the flamingos he saw in Peru.

> **AREA:** 1,285,220 sq km (496,226 sq miles)
> **POPULATION:** 34,683,000
> **CAPITAL CITY:** Lima
> **MAIN LANGUAGES:** Spanish, Quechua

Bolivia (South America)

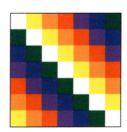 

The stripes on Bolivia's flag (right) stand for the blood shed fighting for independence (red), its mineral wealth (yellow), and its fertile land (green). Bolivia also flies a patchwork rainbow flag, the *Wiphala*, to represent its native Andean peoples.
Similar: Lithuania (18), Ghana (32)

> **AREA:** 1,098,580 sq km (424,164 sq miles)
> **POPULATION:** 12,567,000
> **CAPITAL CITIES:** Sucre, La Paz
> **MAIN LANGUAGES:** Spanish, Quechua, Aymara

Paraguay (South America)

Paraguay's is the only national flag with a different emblem on each side. Its coat of arms is on the front, shown above, and its treasury seal (above right) is on the reverse. **Similar:** Netherlands (19)

> **AREA:** 406,750 sq km (157,047 sq miles)
> **POPULATION:** 6,947,000
> **CAPITAL CITY:** Asunción
> **MAIN LANGUAGES:** Guarani, Spanish

Chile (South America)

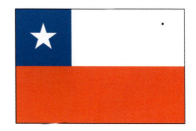

The blue represents the sky, the white stripe is for the snow of the Andes mountains, and the red symbolizes the blood that was spilled fighting for freedom from Spanish rule. The single star stands for progress and dignity.

> **AREA:** 756,950 sq km (292,260 sq miles)
> **POPULATION:** 19,659,000
> **CAPITAL CITY:** Santiago
> **MAIN LANGUAGE:** Spanish

Argentina (South America)

The emblem on this flag is the "Sun of May". It symbolizes a revolution against Spanish rule that began in Argentina and spread to several South American countries in May, 1810. **Similar:** Nicaragua (6)

> **AREA:** 2,776,890 sq km (1,068,302 sq miles)
> **POPULATION:** 46,058,000
> **CAPITAL CITY:** Buenos Aires
> **MAIN LANGUAGE:** Spanish

Uruguay (South America)

This flag features the "Sun of May" (see left) and nine stripes. These stand for the nine counties that made up Uruguay when it won independence from Spain.

> **AREA:** 176,220 sq km (68,039 sq miles)
> **POPULATION:** 3,423,000
> **CAPITAL CITY:** Montevideo
> **MAIN LANGUAGE:** Spanish

Ireland (Northern Europe)

This flag symbolizes peace (white) between the Catholic native people of Gaelic origin (green) and the Protestant British supporters of William of Orange, who settled in Northern Ireland in the 17th century. **Similar:** Ivory Coast (32)

AREA: 70,280 sq km (27,135 sq miles)
POPULATION: 5,089,000
CAPITAL CITY: Dublin
MAIN LANGUAGES: English, Irish (Gaelic)

United Kingdom (Northern Europe)

This is known as the Union Jack or Union Flag. A **jack** is a small flag flown from a naval ship's jackstaff, a short pole at the bow (front). You can read about its history below. To avoid flying it upside-down, note the broad white stripe in the upper hoist, and remember *wide white top*.

AREA: 244,820 sq km (94,526 sq miles)
POPULATION: 67,961,000
CAPITAL CITY: London
MAIN LANGUAGE: English

Flags of the United Kingdom

The Union Jack was created in 1606 when King James I of England and Scotland combined the Scottish flag, St Andrew's Cross, with England's St George's Cross. When Ireland joined Great Britain to form the United Kingdom in 1801, the cross of Ireland's patron saint, Patrick, was added to the flag. England and Wales were already united in King James's day, so Wales has no distinct part in the Union Jack. But the Welsh proudly fly their own flag, too: *Y Ddraig Goch* – The Red Dragon.

Y Ddraig Goch

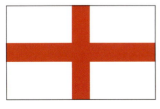
St George's Cross

St Andrew's Cross

St Patrick's Cross

15

Iceland (Nordic countries)

All the national flags of the Nordic countries feature a cross, inspired by Denmark's flag (see opposite). Red symbolizes Iceland's fiery volcanoes, white its ice and snow, and blue its mountains. **Similar:** Norway

AREA: 103,000 sq km (39,769 sq miles)
POPULATION: 378,000
CAPITAL CITY: Reykjavík
MAIN LANGUAGE: Icelandic

Faroe Islands (Nordic countries)

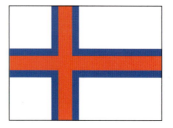

Lying between Iceland and Scotland, the Faroe Islands belong to the Kingdom of Denmark. Their flag was inspired by the red and blue cross designs of fellow Nordic countries Norway and Iceland. White stands for the Faroes' clear, bright sky.

AREA: 1,399 sq km (540 sq miles)
POPULATION: 53,000
CAPITAL CITY: Tórshavn
MAIN LANGUAGES: Faroese, Danish

Norway (Nordic countries)

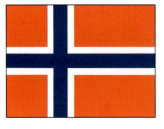

Fredrik Meltzer, the designer of Norway's flag, chose red, white and blue to connect it with the French (18), Dutch (19), American (4) and British (15) flags, which stand for unity and democracy. **Similar:** Iceland, Denmark

AREA: 323,802 sq km (135,021 sq miles)
POPULATION: 5,515,000
CAPITAL CITY: Oslo
MAIN LANGUAGE: Norwegian

Sweden (Nordic countries)

In 1569, King John III of Sweden decreed that his battle banner should have a golden cross. This made its way onto the national flag. The blue and yellow probably come from Sweden's royal emblem, which has three golden crowns on a blue background.

AREA: 449,964 sq km (173,732 sq miles)
POPULATION: 10,674,000
CAPITAL CITY: Stockholm
MAIN LANGUAGE: Swedish

Finland (Nordic countries)

This flag design was proposed in 1862, while Finland was under Russian rule with no flag of its own. The white represents snow, and the blue, Finland's many lakes. The flag was finally flown in 1918, after Finland became independent from Russia.

AREA: 338,145 sq km (130,559 sq miles)
POPULATION: 5,550,000
CAPITAL CITY: Helsinki
MAIN LANGUAGES: Finnish, Swedish

Denmark (Nordic countries)

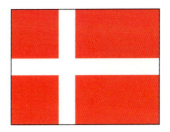

One of the oldest flags, legend says it fell from Heaven at a battle in 1219. The story goes that the Christian Danish King, Valdemar II, who was fighting the pagan Estonians, caught the flag and won the day.
Nickname: *Dannebrog*. **Similar:** Switzerland (19)

AREA: 43,094 sq km (16,639 sq miles)
POPULATION: 5,940,000
CAPITAL CITY: Copenhagen
MAIN LANGUAGE: Danish

Estonia (Northern Europe)

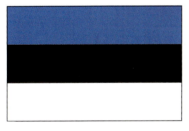

This flag is nicknamed *Sinimustvalge* – blue-black-white in Estonian. It became official on Estonia's independence in 1918. The flag represents Estonia's blue sky and lakes, its dark forests and black, fertile soil, and its white winter snows.

AREA: 45,226 sq km (17,462 sq miles)
POPULATION: 1,319,000
CAPITAL CITY: Tallinn
MAIN LANGUAGES: Estonian, Russian

Latvia (Northern Europe)

This flag was first used in 1918 when Latvia became free from Russian rule. Based on a banner used by 13th-century Latvian soldiers, the design symbolizes the willingness of Latvians to give their hearts' blood (crimson) for their freedom (white). **Similar:** Austria (20)

AREA: 64,589 sq km (24,938 sq miles)
POPULATION: 1,810,000
CAPITAL CITY: Riga
MAIN LANGUAGES: Latvian, Russian

Lithuania (Northern Europe)

This flag was created in 1918, based on Lithuania's traditional costume. In 1944, the Soviet Union took control of the country, banning its flag. When Lithuania became independent in 1989, the flag was flown again. **Similar:** Bolivia (13)

> **AREA:** 65,300 sq km (25,212 sq miles)
> **POPULATION:** 2,693,000
> **CAPITAL CITY:** Vilnius
> **MAIN LANGUAGES:** Lithuanian, Russian

France (Western Europe)

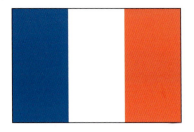

This influential flag is known as the *Tricolore*. It was first used in 1794, after a revolution took place to overthrow the French monarchy. It symbolizes the principles of the revolution – liberty, equality and togetherness.

> **AREA:** 547,030 sq km (211,209 sq miles)
> **POPULATION:** 64,882,000
> **CAPITAL CITY:** Paris
> **MAIN LANGUAGE:** French

Belgium (Western Europe)

The black-gold-red relate to the coat of arms of the medieval Duchy of Brabant. It had a black shield and a gold lion with a red tongue and claws. The official proportions (13:15) are shown here, but most Belgian flags are 2:3 (see 45, *Flag proportions*).

> **AREA:** 30,528 sq km (11,787 sq miles)
> **POPULATION:** 11,716,000
> **CAPITAL CITY:** Brussels
> **MAIN LANGUAGES:** Dutch, French, German

Luxembourg (Western Europe)

Luxembourg didn't have an official flag until 1972. The red, white and blue come from the coat of arms that belonged to the country's Grand Duke in the 13th century.
Similar: Netherlands, Russia (27)

> **AREA:** 2,586 sq km (998 sq miles)
> **POPULATION:** 662,000
> **CAPITAL CITY:** Luxembourg City
> **MAIN LANGUAGES:** Luxembourgish, German, French

Netherlands (Western Europe)

The top stripe was originally orange, for the Dutch rulers, the House of Orange. Over time it was changed to red, but you may still see orange pennants flown alongside the flag on special occasions. **Similar:** Luxembourg

> **AREA:** 41,526 sq km (16,023 sq miles)
> **POPULATION:** 17,671,000
> **CAPITAL CITY:** Amsterdam
> **MAIN LANGUAGE:** Dutch

Monaco (Western Europe)

The red and white come from the coat of arms of the Grimaldis, Monaco's royal family. They first ruled this tiny city-state in the 13th century, and still rule it today, alongside an elected parliament.
Similar: Poland (24), Indonesia (56)

> **AREA:** 1.95 sq km (0.75 sq miles)
> **POPULATION:** 36,000
> **MAIN LANGUAGES:** French, Monegasque, Italian

Germany (Western Europe)

First used in 1848, this flag's black, red and gold stripes were inspired by the uniforms of German soldiers fighting against French Emperor Napoleon in the early 19th century. **Similar:** Belgium

> **AREA:** 357,021 sq km (137,847 sq miles)
> **POPULATION:** 83,252,000
> **CAPITAL CITY:** Berlin
> **MAIN LANGUAGE:** German

Switzerland (Western Europe)

This flag symbolizes faith and freedom. Its origin lies in the medieval war flag of the allied cantons (states) that make up Switzerland. It is one of only two square national flags (see also the Vatican, 21). It inspired the symbol of the Red Cross movement (see 63).

> **AREA:** 41,290 sq km (15,942 sq miles)
> **POPULATION:** 8,851,000
> **CAPITAL CITY:** Bern
> **MAIN LANGUAGES:** German, French, Italian

Liechtenstein (Western Europe)

At the 1936 Summer Olympics, Liechtenstein and Haiti (8) discovered that their red and blue flags were easily confused with each other. So in 1937, the Liechtenstein government added a crown to their flag to make it more distinct.

AREA: 160 sq km (62 sq miles)
POPULATION: 40,000
CAPITAL CITY: Vaduz
MAIN LANGUAGE: German

Austria (Western Europe)

Legend tells of an Austrian Duke who fought in a series of wars known as the Crusades. He lost his banner in battle, so instead, he raised his blood-soaked tunic, with a white stripe left by his belt. It became his official banner, later inspiring Austria's flag. **Similar:** Latvia (17)

AREA: 83,870 sq km (32,382 sq miles)
POPULATION: 8,977,000
CAPITAL CITY: Vienna
MAIN LANGUAGE: German

Portugal (Southern Europe)

The national coat of arms on this flag sits on a yellow armillary sphere. This was a navigational instrument used by Portuguese explorers sailing across the world during the 15th–17th centuries.

AREA: 92,391 sq km (35,672 sq miles)
POPULATION: 10,223,000
CAPITAL CITY: Lisbon
MAIN LANGUAGE: Portuguese

Spain (Southern Europe)

The coat of arms shows a red banner displaying the words *Plus ultra*, Latin for *Further beyond*. This was the motto of Spanish king Charles V, who built an empire far beyond Spain in the 16th century.

AREA: 504,750 sq km (194,897 sq miles)
POPULATION: 47,473,000
CAPITAL CITY: Madrid
MAIN LANGUAGES: Castilian Spanish, Catalan

Italy (Southern Europe)

Italy's flag was inspired by France's (18). Green-white-red flags were first used in northern Italy when it was ruled by French emperor Napoleon. The design was taken up by Italy as a whole when it was united into a single country in 1861. **Similar:** Mexico (5)

> **AREA:** 301,230 sq km (116,306 sq miles)
> **POPULATION:** 58,698,000
> **CAPITAL CITY:** Rome
> **MAIN LANGUAGE:** Italian

Andorra (Southern Europe)

Landlocked between France (18) and Spain, this tiny mountain nation has a flag that reflects theirs. At the bottom of the coat of arms is the Latin motto *Virtus unita fortior* – strength united is stronger. **Similar:** Moldova (26), Romania (26), Chad (34)

> **AREA:** 468 sq km (181 sq miles)
> **POPULATION:** 80,000
> **CAPITAL CITY:** Andorra la Vella
> **MAIN LANGUAGES:** Catalan, Spanish

San Marino (Southern Europe)

San Marino is a tiny country that lies entirely inside Italy. The coat of arms on its flag shows the three peaks of Monte Titano, and their three fortresses, which once guarded San Marino's capital city. The word *Libertas* on the scroll is Latin for *Freedom*.

> **AREA:** 160 sq km (62 sq miles)
> **POPULATION:** 34,000
> **CAPITAL CITY:** San Marino
> **MAIN LANGUAGE:** Italian

Vatican City State (Southern Europe)

The Vatican, in Rome, Italy, is the world's smallest nation. It is the home of the Pope, the head of the Catholic Church. This square flag (see Switzerland, 19) shows a crown that popes used to wear, and the keys to Heaven.

> **AREA:** 0.44 sq km (0.17 sq miles)
> **POPULATION:** 520
> **MAIN LANGUAGES:** Italian, Latin

Slovenia (Southern Europe)

The coat of arms shows the three peaks of Triglav, Slovenia's highest mountain. The wavy blue lines stand for Slovenia's rivers and the Adriatic Sea. The triangle of golden stars is from the coat of arms of a medieval ruling family.
Similar: Slovakia (25), Russia (27)

> **AREA:** 20,273 sq km (7,827 sq miles)
> **POPULATION:** 2,118,000
> **CAPITAL CITY:** Ljubljana
> **MAIN LANGUAGE:** Slovenian

Malta (Southern Europe)

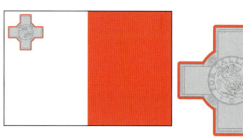

The symbol in the corner shows the George Cross, the highest non-military award for gallantry in the UK. British king George VI awarded one to the people of Malta in 1942, for their outstanding bravery during the Second World War.

> **AREA:** 316 sq km (122 sq miles)
> **POPULATION:** 537,000
> **CAPITAL CITY:** Valletta
> **MAIN LANGUAGES:** Maltese, English

Croatia (Southern Europe)

The check-patterned coat of arms comes from Stephen Držislav, a 10th-century Croatian king. Legend says he was captured by the Venetians but won his freedom by beating their ruler Pietro II in a chess match. **Similar:** Paraguay (14)

> **AREA:** 56,542 sq km (21,831 sq miles)
> **POPULATION:** 3,987,000
> **CAPITAL CITY:** Zagreb
> **MAIN LANGUAGE:** Croatian

Serbia (Southern Europe)

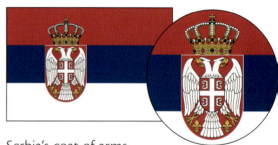

Serbia's coat of arms includes the Byzantine two-headed eagle (see Albania, 24). In the middle are four letter-like symbols, said to stand for a Serbian phrase that means *Only unity saves the Serbs*. **Similar:** Slovakia (25)

> **AREA:** 77,474 sq km (29,913 sq miles)
> **POPULATION:** 7,097,000
> **CAPITAL CITY:** Belgrade
> **MAIN LANGUAGES:** Serbian, Hungarian

Bosnia and Herzegovina
(Southern Europe)

In 1995, the United Nations (see 63) helped the warring Bosniaks, Serbs and Croats to form a new nation. They couldn't agree on a flag, so in 1998 the UN chose this. The triangle represents the country's shape and its three peoples. The blue and stars are for Europe.

AREA: 51,209 sq km (19,772 sq miles)
POPULATION: 3,194,000
CAPITAL CITY: Sarajevo
MAIN LANGUAGES: Bosnian, Serbian, Croatian

Montenegro (Southern Europe)

This flag was officially raised in 2006 when Montenegro became independent from Serbia, although it had already been in use for two years. It's based on a banner used by Montenegro's only king, Nikola I, who ruled from 1910 to 1918.

AREA: 14,026 sq km (5,415 sq miles)
POPULATION: 626,000
CAPITAL CITY: Podgorica
MAIN LANGUAGES: Serbian, Montenegrin

Greece (Southern Europe)

Here, the blue and white stand for the sea and waves. The nine stripes are said to represent the syllables of Greece's motto, *Eleftheria i thanatos*, which means *Freedom or death*. The cross reflects Greece's Christian heritage.

AREA: 131,940 sq km (50,942 sq miles)
POPULATION: 10,301,000
CAPITAL CITY: Athens
MAIN LANGUAGE: Greek

North Macedonia (Southern Europe)

Macedonia, as it was then known, broke away from Yugoslavia in 1991–1992. This, its second flag, was first used in 1995. It is red and yellow, from the country's old coat of arms, and illustrates a line of its national anthem: *Today over Macedonia is born the new sun of liberty*.

AREA: 25,333 sq km (9,781 sq miles)
POPULATION: 2,083,000
CAPITAL CITY: Skopje
MAIN LANGUAGES: Macedonian, Albanian

Albania (Southern Europe)

The two-headed eagle is a symbol of the ancient Byzantine Empire. It was used by the Albanian hero Skanderbeg, who defended the nation against Turkish invaders in the 1440s. Albanians call their country *Shqipëria*, which means *Land of the Eagle*.

AREA: 28,748 sq km (11,100 sq miles)
POPULATION: 2,826,000
CAPITAL CITY: Tirana
MAIN LANGUAGE: Albanian

Kosovo (Southern Europe)

In 2008, Kosovo declared independence from Serbia (22), and a competition was launched to design a new national flag. This winning entry reflected the European Union flag (see 63). Above the country's outline are six stars to represent its main people groups.

AREA: 10,887 sq km (4,203 sq miles)
POPULATION: 1,667,000
CAPITAL CITY: Pristina
MAIN LANGUAGES: Albanian, Serbian, Bosnian

Poland (Eastern Europe)

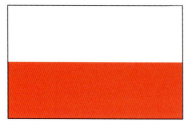

Polish children are taught a song about their national flag, which includes the lines: *And on this flag there's white and red. Red for love, white for a pure heart.*
Similar: Indonesia (56), Monaco (19)

AREA: 313,679 sq km (120,726 sq miles)
POPULATION: 40,222,000
CAPITAL CITY: Warsaw
MAIN LANGUAGE: Polish

Czechia (Eastern Europe)

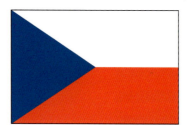

This was the flag of Czechoslovakia. Red and white are from the coat of arms of Bohemia, in the west; blue is from the arms of Slovakia. It also reflects the Pan-Slavic flag (see 27). In 1993, Czechoslovakia split into Slovakia and the Czech Republic, or Czechia, which kept the old flag. **Similar:** Philippines (56)

AREA: 78,866 sq km (30,450 sq miles)
POPULATION: 10,504,000
CAPITAL CITY: Prague
MAIN LANGUAGE: Czech

Slovakia (Eastern Europe)

The Slovak coat of arms shows an Orthodox Christian cross. The hills it stands on symbolize the three mountain ranges where the Slovak people originally lived. **Similar:** Slovenia (22), Russia (27)

AREA: 48,845 sq km (18,859 sq miles)
POPULATION: 5,703,000
CAPITAL CITY: Bratislava
MAIN LANGUAGES: Slovak, Hungarian

Hungary (Eastern Europe)

This flag was first flown in a failed revolution against the Austrian Empire in 1848. Its red-white-green came from Hungary's coat of arms. The three-stripe design was inspired by the French flag (18).

AREA: 93,030 sq km (35,919 sq miles)
POPULATION: 9,995,000
CAPITAL CITY: Budapest
MAIN LANGUAGE: Hungarian

Flags and heraldry

Many national flags have their origins in heraldry: the coats of arms displayed on shields and banners by the monarchs and nobles of Europe. If you look at the flags of these countries, you can see how their combinations of red, white, and other elements were based on the ancient coats of arms below.

Poland

Slovakia

Hungary

Belarus (Eastern Europe)

In 1951, Belarus was part of the Soviet Union and first flew this flag with a hammer and sickle emblem on it (see 52). The hoist pattern represents purity and joy in Belarusian culture. On independence in 1991, the country briefly used a different flag, but in 1995 the red-green flag returned, minus the Soviet emblem.

AREA: 207,600 sq km (80,155 sq miles)
POPULATION: 9,455,000
CAPITAL CITY: Minsk
MAIN LANGUAGE: Belarusian

Ukraine (Eastern Europe)

The blue and yellow were originally taken from a Ukrainian coat of arms that showed a golden lion on a blue shield. These days, the stripes are seen as symbolizing a blue sky over golden wheatfields. Always a top wheat producer, Ukraine has been nicknamed *the breadbasket of Europe*.

AREA: 603,700 sq km (233,090 sq miles)
POPULATION: 37,938,000
CAPITAL CITY: Kyiv
MAIN LANGUAGES: Ukrainian, Russian

Moldova (Eastern Europe)

Until the Second World War, Moldova was part of Romania. The Moldovan coat of arms features an eagle and the head of a wild ox, representing Wallachia and Moldavia, historical regions of Romania and Moldova. **Similar:** Romania, Andorra (21)

AREA: 33,843 sq km (13,067 sq miles)
POPULATION: 3,330,000
CAPITAL CITY: Chisinau
MAIN LANGUAGE: Moldovan (Romanian)

Romania (Eastern Europe)

The stripes stand for liberty (blue), justice (yellow) and togetherness (red). They were used on royal Romanian shields and banners during the late 16th century. This flag is identical to that of Chad (34) except for a slightly different shade of blue.

AREA: 237,500 sq km (91,699 sq miles)
POPULATION: 19,619,000
CAPITAL CITY: Bucharest
MAIN LANGUAGE: Romanian

Bulgaria (Eastern Europe)

This flag was first used in 1879. Like many Slavic flags (see below), its design was inspired by Russia's flag, but a green stripe replaced the blue to represent freedom. In 1947, the national coat of arms was placed in the top left corner, but was removed again in 1990. **Similar:** Hungary (25)

AREA: 110,910 sq km (42,823 sq miles)
POPULATION: 6,617,000
CAPITAL CITY: Sofia
MAIN LANGUAGE: Bulgarian

Russia (Eastern Europe and Asia)

In the late 1690s, Peter the Great, Tsar of Russia, visited dockyards in the Netherlands to learn about shipbuilding. He created a modern flag for Russia in the horizontal tri-band style of the Dutch flag (19) with the red-white-blue of Moscow's coat of arms.

AREA: 17,075,200 sq km (7,592,772 sq miles)
POPULATION: 143,957,000
CAPITAL CITY: Moscow
MAIN LANGUAGE: Russian

The Pan-Slavic flag

The Slavic peoples mostly come from Eastern and Central Europe. In 1848, a year of great turmoil in Europe, Slavs from many nations gathered in Prague, in what is now Czechia (24). They met to discuss the threat of a new German Empire. At that meeting, a new Pan-Slavic flag was raised to represent all Slavic peoples – *pan* means *all*. It was inspired by the Russian flag.

The Pan-Slavic flag became the first flag of the Kingdom of Yugoslavia (1918–1943). It inspired the flags of former Yugoslav countries including Slovenia, Croatia and Serbia (22), and others, such as Bulgaria, Czechia (24) and Slovakia (25).

Tunisia (North Africa)

This red flag with a star and crescent recalls a time when Tunisia was part of the Ottoman Empire (see below). The emblem also echoes the crescent banners of ancient Carthage (near Tunis) which symbolized its patron goddess, Tanit.

AREA: 163,610 sq km (63,170 sq miles)
POPULATION: 12,565,000
CAPITAL CITY: Tunis
MAIN LANGUAGES: Arabic, French

Algeria (North Africa)

Green and white are said to be inspired by the flag of Abd al-Qadir, an Algerian hero who fought the French in the 19th century. The star and crescent are symbols of Islam, from the time when Algeria was part of the Ottoman Empire (see below).

AREA: 2,381,740 sq km (919,595 sq miles)
POPULATION: 46,279,000
CAPITAL CITY: Algiers
MAIN LANGUAGES: Arabic, French, Berber dialects

The star and crescent

The Islamic Ottoman Empire started in what is now Turkey (42), and lasted for over 600 years. At the height of its power, in the 16th and 17th centuries, it stretched from Hungary to Ethiopia, and from the Caspian Sea to Algeria. It had many flags over the centuries, but after conquering Constantinople, now Istanbul, in 1453, it flew one bearing a crescent, the city's symbol. This ancient Western Asian emblem, often coupled with a star, has become the most famous symbol of Islam.

The Ottoman and Turkish flags have inspired those of many Muslim countries, including Tunisia, Algeria, Libya, Mauritania (30), Azerbaijan (47), Turkmenistan (47) and Pakistan (49).

Morocco (North Africa)

The red is from the flag of the Alaouites, Morocco's royal family. In 1912, a six-pointed star, Solomon's Seal, an old symbol of life, was added. It was changed to a five-pointed star in 1915. To Moroccans, this represents the Five Pillars (duties) of Islam.

AREA: 446,550 sq km (172,414 sq miles)
POPULATION: 38,211,000
CAPITAL CITY: Rabat
MAIN LANGUAGES: Arabic, Berber, French

Libya (North Africa)

This flag first flew when Libya was united in 1951. It was replaced by a plain green flag under the rule of Muammar Gaddafi from 1969, but restored when a new government took power in 2011. The red, black and green represent the regions of Fezzan, Cyrenaica and Tripolitania.

AREA: 1,759,540 sq km (679,362 sq miles)
POPULATION: 6,964,000
CAPITAL CITY: Tripoli
MAIN LANGUAGES: Arabic, Berber dialects, English

Egypt (North Africa)

Egypt's flag gives a new meaning to the Pan-Arab red-white-black (see 43). Black is the dark past under foreign rule; white the bright future; red the struggle to get there. The eagle is the emblem of Saladin, a 12th-century ruler of Egypt and Syria.

AREA: 1,001,450 sq km (386,662 sq miles)
POPULATION: 114,484,000
CAPITAL CITY: Cairo
MAIN LANGUAGE: Arabic

Sudan (North Africa)

Like Egypt, Sudan's flag was inspired by the Pan-Arab flag (43). The red stands for the struggle for independence; the white for peace; the black for Sudan itself, whose name means "black". The green triangle stands for Islam.

AREA: 1,886,068 sq km (728,215 sq miles)
POPULATION: 49,358,000
CAPITAL CITY: Khartoum
MAIN LANGUAGES: Arabic, English, Beja

Mauritania (North Africa)

The green and gold are inspired by Pan-African ideas (see Ghana, 32). Green stands for Islam, too. The star and crescent are also Islamic symbols (see 28). The crescent moon is on its back, as it's seen in the sky above Mauritania. **Similar:** Pakistan (49)

AREA: 1,030,700 sq km (397,955 sq miles)
POPULATION: 4,944,000
CAPITAL CITY: Nouakchott
MAIN LANGUAGES: Arabic, Wolof, French

Cape Verde (West Africa)

The circle of ten stars represents the ten islands that make up Cape Verde. The blue stands for the sea and sky. The white is for peace, the red is for hard work, and together they make a road, symbolizing the path to building a new country.

AREA: 4,033 sq km (1,577 sq miles)
POPULATION: 604,000
CAPITAL CITY: Praia
MAIN LANGUAGES: Crioulo, Portuguese

Senegal (West Africa)

Senegal was once united with Mali (32) and its flag is identical apart from the star, symbolizing unity and hope. Green stands for Islam, gold for wealth through hard work, and red for past struggles.
Similar: Guinea, Cameroon (34)

AREA: 196,190 sq km (75,749 sq miles)
POPULATION: 18,222,000
CAPITAL CITY: Dakar
MAIN LANGUAGES: Wolof, French, Pulaar

The Gambia (West Africa)

Red symbolizes the Gambia's hot sun and rolling savannah. Blue stands for the Gambia River, along whose banks the country lies, and from which it takes its name. Green represents the country's forests. The white stripes stand for unity and peace.

AREA: 11,300 sq km (4,363 sq miles)
POPULATION: 2,842,000
CAPITAL CITY: Banjul
MAIN LANGUAGES: Mandinka, Fulu, Wolof, English

Guinea (West Africa)

Guinea was once ruled by France, and it was the first of its colonies to become independent, in 1958. Its flag was inspired by the French *Tricolore* (18) and the Pan-African flag of Ghana (32). **Similar:** Mali (32)

AREA: 245,857 sq km (94,925 sq miles)
POPULATION: 14,529,000
CAPITAL CITY: Conakry
MAIN LANGUAGES: Fulu, Maninka, Susu, French

Guinea-Bissau (West Africa)

This Pan-African flag* comes from the political party that won the country's independence from Portugal in 1973. Red symbolizes past suffering. Yellow signifies wealth through hard work, and green stands for forests and hope. The black star represents Africa.

AREA: 36,120 sq km (13,946 sq miles)
POPULATION: 2,197,000
CAPITAL CITY: Bissau
MAIN LANGUAGES: Crioulo, Portuguese, Fula, Balanta, French, Mandinka, Mandjak

*See Ghana, 32

Sierra Leone (West Africa)

The green-white-blue stripes were inspired by the country's coat of arms, which features green hills above blue and white ocean waves. Green also stands for farming, white for unity and justice, and blue for the hope of peace.

AREA: 71,740 sq km (27,699 sq miles)
POPULATION: 8,978,000
CAPITAL CITY: Freetown
MAIN LANGUAGES: Krio, English, Mende, Temne

Liberia (West Africa)

Liberia was founded as a refuge for people formerly enslaved in America. Its flag is based on the Stars and Stripes (4). Originally, the flag had a white cross in the corner. This was changed to a star in 1847, when Liberia became independent from the USA. **Nickname:** The Lone Star

AREA: 111,370 sq km (43,000 sq miles)
POPULATION: 5,537,000
CAPITAL CITY: Monrovia
MAIN LANGUAGES: English, Kreyol, Kpelle, Bassa

Mali (West Africa)

Green stands for the land; gold for the local gold mines; red for blood shed defending Mali. The flag once had a black human figure in the middle. This was removed because Islam, the national religion, forbids images of people. **Similar:** Senegal (30), Guinea (31)

> **AREA:** 1,240,000 sq km (478,767 sq miles)
> **POPULATION:** 24,016,000
> **CAPITAL CITY:** Bamako
> **MAIN LANGUAGES:** Bambara, Soninke, Fula, Maninka, Songhai, French

Ivory Coast (West Africa)

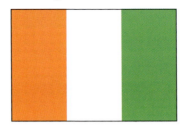

The flag was inspired by the *Tricolore* flag of France (18), who ruled the country when it was at the heart of the trade in ivory from elephant tusks. Orange stands for the land, white for peace and justice, and green for hope. **Similar:** Ireland (15)

> **AREA:** 322,460 sq km (124,503 sq miles)
> **POPULATION:** 29,603,000
> **CAPITAL CITY:** Yamoussoukro
> **MAIN LANGUAGES:** French, Baoule, Dioula

Burkina Faso (West Africa)

In this Pan-African design, inspired by Ghana's (right), red symbolizes the country's struggle to transform itself. Green stands for its fertile land. The star reflects socialist ideas about revolution (see note at foot of 52).

> **AREA:** 274,200 sq km (105,869 sq miles)
> **POPULATION:** 23,840,000
> **CAPITAL CITY:** Ouagadougou
> **MAIN LANGUAGES:** Mooré, Fula, French

Ghana (West Africa)

A new nation in 1957, Ghana's flag was inspired by Ethiopia's (36). Red stood for the struggle for independence; gold for Ghana's wealth*; green for its forests. Its **Black Star of Africa**** is a symbol of African freedom from the **Pan-African Movement** for independence. The Pan-African **red**, **gold**, **green** and **black** are seen on many African flags.

> **AREA:** 239,460 sq km (92,456 sq miles)
> **POPULATION:** 34,778,000
> **CAPITAL CITY:** Accra
> **MAIN LANGUAGES:** English, Fante, Twi, Dagbani, Pidgin, Ewe

*As a British colony, Ghana was known as the *Gold Coast*, famed for its rich mineral resources.
**It was inspired by the African-run Black Star Shipping Line started by Black leader Marcus Garvey in 1919.

Togo (West Africa)

This Pan-African flag (see Ghana) was also inspired by the US-style flag of Liberia (31). Red stands for blood shed defending Togo. Green is for hope. Gold signifies the precious value of unity, and the white star symbolizes peace and life.

AREA: 56,785 sq km (21,925 sq miles)
POPULATION: 9,261,000
CAPITAL CITY: Lomé
MAIN LANGUAGES: Mina, Ewe, Kabye, French

Benin (West Africa)

The meaning of Benin's flag appears in its national anthem: *In the green you read the hope of revival; The red recalls the courage of your ancestors; The yellow foretells the richest treasures.*

AREA: 112,620 sq km (43,483 sq miles)
POPULATION: 14,080,000
CAPITAL CITY: Porto-Novo
MAIN LANGUAGES: Fon, French, Yoruba, Adja

Niger (West Africa)

Orange represents the Sahara Desert, which covers most of Niger. Green is for the lush plains in the south, fed by the River Niger. White stands for purity and hope. The orange circle represents the sun. **Similar**: India (49)

AREA: 1,267,000 sq km (489,191 sq miles)
POPULATION: 28,239,000
CAPITAL CITY: Niamey
MAIN LANGUAGES: Hausa, Djerma, French

Nigeria (West Africa)

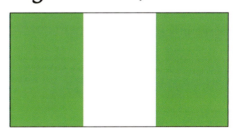

The green in Nigeria's flag represents farming and forests. Before it discovered oil, Nigeria made most of its money from farmed goods such as peanuts and palm oil. Even today, more than a third of Nigerians are farmers. The white band symbolizes peace.

AREA: 923,768 sq km (356,669 sq miles)
POPULATION: 229,152,000
CAPITAL CITY: Abuja
MAIN LANGUAGES: English, Pidgin, Hausa, Yoruba, Igbo, Fula

Chad (Central Africa)

This design combines the flag of Chad's former rulers, France (18) with the Pan-African gold (see Ghana, 32). Blue stands for hope, gold for the desert sun, and red for progress. **Similar:** Romania (26)

AREA: 1,284,000 sq km (495,755 sq miles)
POPULATION: 18,847,000
CAPITAL CITY: N'Djamena
MAIN LANGUAGES: Arabic, French, Sara

Cameroon (Central Africa)

Cameroon was the first country to follow Ghana (32) in creating a Pan-African style flag. The three vertical stripes recall the time when France (18) ruled Cameroon. Green, red and yellow stand for hope, unity and sunshine. **Similar:** Senegal (30)

AREA: 475,440 sq km (183,568 sq miles)
POPULATION: 29,394,000
CAPITAL CITY: Yaoundé
MAIN LANGUAGES: Cameroon Pidgin, French, English, Fula, Bulu, Ewondo

Equatorial Guinea
(Central Africa)

The coat of arms on the flag shows a silk cotton tree beneath which the people of Equatorial Guinea first signed a treaty with their former ruler, Spain. The six yellow stars stand for the mainland and islands that make up the country.

AREA: 28,050 sq km (10,831 sq miles)
POPULATION: 1,755,000
CAPITAL CITY: Malabo
MAIN LANGUAGES: Spanish, Fang, Portuguese

Sao Tome and Principe
(Central Africa)

This Pan-African style flag (see Ghana, 32) has a star for each of the country's two islands. Red stands for the blood shed in the struggle for independence. Green is for the fertile land. Yellow stands for the yellow pods of cocoa beans, the country's main crop.

AREA: 964 sq km (372 sq miles)
POPULATION: 237,000
CAPITAL CITY: São Tomé
MAIN LANGUAGES: Portuguese, Crioulo dialects

Gabon (Central Africa)

This flag was first flown in 1960. The yellow stripe represents Gabon's position on the Equator, an imaginary line around the middle of the Earth. The green is for forests and the blue for the Atlantic Ocean.

AREA: 267,667 sq km (103,347 sq miles)
POPULATION: 2,485,000
CAPITAL CITY: Libreville
MAIN LANGUAGES: French, Fang, Myene

Central African Republic

The Central African Republic shows its joint French-African heritage by combining the blue-white-red of France's flag (18) with the Pan-African green-gold-red (see Ghana, 32). The red band stands for the blood that everyone shares, black or white.

AREA: 622,984 sq km (240,535 sq miles)
POPULATION: 5,916,000
CAPITAL CITY: Bangui
MAIN LANGUAGES: Sangho, French

Republic of the Congo
(Central Africa)

The diagonal design sets it apart from all other Pan-African flags (see Ghana, 32). Green stands for farming and forests, yellow for the friendship and nobility of the Congolese people, and red for the blood common to all people.

AREA: 342,000 sq km (132,047 sq miles)
POPULATION: 6,245,000
CAPITAL CITY: Brazzaville
MAIN LANGUAGES: French, Munukutuba, Lingala

D R Congo
(Central Africa)

The Democratic Republic of the Congo has a flag with a sky-blue background, symbolizing peace. Red stands for the blood shed for the country. Gold represents wealth, and the star its shining future. The country used to be called Zaïre, and had a green flag with a fiery torch.

AREA: 2,345,410 sq km (905,568 sq miles)
POPULATION: 105,625,000
CAPITAL CITY: Kinshasa
MAIN LANGUAGES: French, Kikongo, Lingala, Swahili, Tshiluba, Kingwana

Eritrea (East Africa)

The yellow emblem is a sprouting olive wreath, inspired by the United Nations flag (63). By law, the Eritrean flag must be deeply respected. For example, a driver who sees it being hoisted must park the car, get out and stand still until the flag is fully raised.

AREA: 117,600 sq km (45,406 sq miles)
POPULATION: 3,818,000
CAPITAL CITY: Asmara
MAIN LANGUAGES: Tigrinya, Afar, Arabic

South Sudan (East Africa)

South Sudan became independent from Sudan in 2011. Black represents its people; red, its struggle for independence; green, its natural wealth. The white stripes represent peace. The blue triangle is for the River Nile, and the gold star stands for unity. **Similar**: Kenya, Sudan (29)

AREA: 619,745 sq km (239,285 sq miles)
POPULATION: 11,277,000
CAPITAL CITY: Juba
MAIN LANGUAGES: English, Arabic

Ethiopia (East Africa)

Ethiopia is Africa's oldest independent nation. The green-gold-red of its flag comes from the war pennants of the old Ethiopian Empire (see feature, 50). It has inspired the flags of many other African countries (see Ghana, 32). The star emblem with rays stands for democratic hope and equality.

AREA: 1,127,127 sq km (435,186 sq miles)
POPULATION: 129,720,000
CAPITAL CITY: Addis Ababa
MAIN LANGUAGES: Amharic, Tigrinya, Arabic

Djibouti (East Africa)

In Djibouti's flag, blue stands for the sea and sky, green is for the earth, and white is for peace. Blue and green also represent the country's two main peoples, the Somalis and the Afar. The red star symbolizes unity and the blood shed in the fight for independence.

AREA: 23,000 sq km (8,880 sq miles)
POPULATION: 1,152,000
CAPITAL CITY: Djibouti City
MAIN LANGUAGES: Somali, Afar, Arabic, French

Somalia (East Africa)

This flag was inspired by that of the United Nations (63), which helped run Somalia until it reached independence in 1960. The five points of the star stand for five parts of Africa where Somalis live, including parts of Kenya and Djibouti.

AREA: 637,657 sq km (246,201 sq miles)
POPULATION: 18,707,000
CAPITAL CITY: Mogadishu
MAIN LANGUAGES: Somali, Arabic, Oromo

Kenya (East Africa)

Kenya's Pan-African flag* shows the traditional shield and spears of its native Maasai people. Black stands for the Black peoples of Kenya. Red is for the struggle for independence. Green is for the country's natural riches. The white stripes symbolize peace.

AREA: 582,650 sq km (224,962 sq miles)
POPULATION: 56,203,000
CAPITAL CITY: Nairobi
MAIN LANGUAGES: Swahili, English, Bantu languages

*See Ghana, 32

Uganda (East Africa)

The black stands for Africa; yellow for sunshine; red for our worldwide human family. The emblem shows an East African crowned crane, Uganda's national bird, which is famed for its gentleness – a quality Ugandans admire.

AREA: 241,083 sq km (93,083 sq miles)
POPULATION: 49,924,000
CAPITAL CITY: Juba
MAIN LANGUAGES: Luganda, English, Swahili

Rwanda (East Africa)

The green in Rwanda's flag symbolizes hope. Yellow represents working together to build a prosperous country. The golden sun signifies the light of understanding. For Rwandans, blue is an important symbol of peace, replacing a red band in their former flag.

AREA: 26,338 sq km (10,169 sq miles)
POPULATION: 14,415,000
CAPITAL CITY: Kigali
MAIN LANGUAGES: Kinyarwanda, French, English, Swahili

Burundi (East Africa)

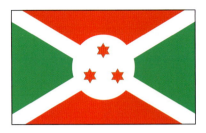

The three stars represent Burundi's national motto, *Unity, work, progress,* and also three local tribes, the Hutu, Tutsi and Twa. Red symbolizes the fight for independence. Green stands for hope, and white is for peace. This flag was first used in 1967.

AREA: 27,830 sq km (10,745 sq miles)
POPULATION: 13,592,000
CAPITAL CITIES: Gitega, Bujumbura
MAIN LANGUAGES: Kirundi, French, Swahili

Tanzania (East Africa)

In 1964, the countries Tanganyika and Zanzibar united to form Tanzania. The flag of Tanganyika was green with a yellow-bordered black stripe. Zanzibar's had bands of blue, black and green. Both designs were combined to create Tanzania's new flag.

AREA: 945,087 sq km (364,900 sq miles)
POPULATION: 69,419,000
CAPITAL CITY: Dodoma
MAIN LANGUAGES: Swahili, English, Sukuma

Comoros (East Africa)

Here, the four stripes represent the islands of Comoros: Mohéli (gold), Mayotte (white), Anjouan (red) and Grand Comore (blue). The green triangle with the crescent and stars symbolizes Islam, the country's main religion (see 28).

AREA: 2,170 sq km (838 sq miles)
POPULATION: 868,000
CAPITAL CITY: Moroni
MAIN LANGUAGES: Comorian, French, Arabic

Seychelles (East Africa)

This flag was first used in 1996. It symbolizes a dynamic young country moving into a bright new future. Blue stands for the sky and sea around the islands. Yellow is for sunshine. Red is for hard work. White represents justice and harmony, and green is for the land.

AREA: 455 sq km (176 sq miles)
POPULATION: 108,000
CAPITAL CITY: Victoria
MAIN LANGUAGES: Seselwa, English

Madagascar (East Africa)

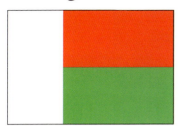

The red and white come from the flag of the Merina Kingdom, which ruled Madagascar in the 18th and 19th centuries. The green stands for the Hova people. They were the peasant class of the Merina Kingdom, and played a big part in the fight for independence.

> **AREA:** 587,040 sq km (226,657 sq miles)
> **POPULATION:** 31,057,000
> **CAPITAL CITY:** Antananarivo
> **MAIN LANGUAGES:** Malagasy, French, Cotiers

Mauritius (East Africa)

The red-blue-yellow-green is from the Mauritian coat of arms. The meanings are said to be red for independence, blue for the Indian Ocean, yellow for a bright future and green for the island's lush vegetation.

> **AREA:** 2,040 sq km (788 sq miles)
> **POPULATION:** 1,302,000
> **CAPITAL CITY:** Port Louis
> **MAIN LANGUAGES:** Mauritian Creole, French, Bhojpuri, English

Malawi (Southern Africa)

Red stands for the blood shed by those who died fighting for Malawi's independence. Black is for the African people. Green is for the rich land. The rising sun symbolizes the dawn of hope and freedom for the whole of Africa.

> **AREA:** 118,480 sq km (45,745 sq miles)
> **POPULATION:** 21,476,000
> **CAPITAL CITY:** Lilongwe
> **MAIN LANGUAGES:** Chichewa, English, Chinyanja

Mozambique (Southern Africa)

In 1975, the Frelimo political party won the country's independence. The party's flag, inspired by South Africa's ANC party (41), became the basis of Mozambique's. The book, hoe and rifle stand for education, farming and self-protection.

> **AREA:** 799,380 sq km (308,642 sq miles)
> **POPULATION:** 34,858,000
> **CAPITAL CITY:** Maputo
> **MAIN LANGUAGES:** Makua, Tsonga, Portuguese, Emskhuwa, Xichangana

Angola (Southern Africa)

Angola's flag is based on that of the political party that won independence from Portugal in 1975. The yellow symbols are a half-cogwheel and a long farmer's knife called a machete. They symbolize factory workers and farmers joined in unity. The star stands for progress.

AREA: 1,246,700 sq km (481,354 sq miles)
POPULATION: 37,801,000
CAPITAL CITY: Luanda
MAIN LANGUAGES: Portuguese, Umbundu, Kikongo, Kimbundu, other Bantu languages

Zambia (Southern Africa)

Zambia's flag is unusual in having its symbols close to the fly edge. The eagle represents rising above troubles. Orange stands for copper, Zambia's main export. Black is for Zambia's people, and red is for their struggle for freedom.

AREA: 752,614 sq km (290,586 sq miles)
POPULATION: 21,135,000
CAPITAL CITY: Lusaka
MAIN LANGUAGES: Bemba, Nyanja, Tonga, English, Kaonde, Lozi, Lunda, Luvale

Zimbabwe (Southern Africa)

The emblem inside the triangle shows a stone statuette of a bird. This was found in the ruins of Great Zimbabwe, an ancient stone city whose walls still stand at 250m (820ft) around. The stripes are a Pan-African design (see Ghana, 32).

AREA: 390,580 sq km (150,804 sq miles)
POPULATION: 17,020,000
CAPITAL CITY: Harare
MAIN LANGUAGES: Shona, Ndebele, English

Namibia (Southern Africa)

On this flag, red stands for the Namibian people. Blue is for the clear sky and the Atlantic Ocean. Green is for the riches of the land. The narrow white stripes represent peace and unity. The sun symbolizes life and energy.

AREA: 825,418 sq km (318,696 sq miles)
POPULATION: 2,675,000
CAPITAL CITY: Windhoek
MAIN LANGUAGES: Oshiwambo dialects, Khoekhoe, Afrikaans, English

Botswana (Southern Africa)

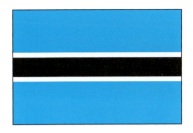

Botswana's flag was inspired by its coat of arms, which features two zebras, and the national motto, *Pula* – Setswana for *Let it rain*. The blue represents longed-for rain, and the black-and-white zebra stripes are a symbol of racial harmony.

AREA: 600,370 sq km (231,804 sq miles)
POPULATION: 2,720,000
CAPITAL CITY: Gaborone
MAIN LANGUAGES: Setswana, Kalanga, English

South Africa (Southern Africa)

In 1994, South Africa's first free elections ended the system of racial segregation called *Apartheid*. This new flag combined old South African flags with that of the the winning political party, the African National Congress. The green "Y" shape symbolizes peoples who were once separate moving ahead together into a new future.

AREA: 1,219,912 sq km (471,011 sq miles)
POPULATION: 61,020,000
CAPITAL CITIES: Pretoria, Bloemfontein, Cape Town
MAIN LANGUAGES: Zulu, Xhosa, Afrikaans, English

Eswatini (Southern Africa)

Eswatini's flag features a traditional shield and two local Assegai spears, decorated with tassels made from the feathers of widowbirds and louries. Red symbolizes past battles, yellow is for the country's wealth and blue is for peace.

AREA: 17,363 sq km (6,704 sq miles)
POPULATION: 1,222,000
CAPITAL CITIES: Mbabane, Lobamba
MAIN LANGUAGES: Swati, English

Lesotho (Southern Africa)

First raised in 2006, the blue-white-green stripes on Lesotho's flag represent rain, peace and prosperity. The emblem is a *mokorotlo*, a type of straw hat traditionally worn by the Basotho people. It is black to symbolize Africa.

AREA: 30,355 sq km (11,720 sq miles)
POPULATION: 2,330,000
CAPITAL CITY: Maseru
MAIN LANGUAGES: Sesotho, English, Zulu, Xhosa

Turkey (Western Asia)

This design is based closely on the flag of the Ottoman Empire (see 28). A popular legend about the origins of this ancient flag says that during the Battle of Kosovo in 1448, a crescent moon and star were seen reflected in pools of blood.

> AREA: 780,580 sq km (301,384 sq miles)
> POPULATION: 86,260,000
> CAPITAL CITY: Ankara
> MAIN LANGUAGE: Turkish

Cyprus (Western Asia)

The white background and olive branches symbolize the hope of peace between Greek and Turkish Cypriots. The orange map represents the copper that has been mined in Cyprus since ancient times. The word "copper" means "metal of Cyprus."

> AREA: 9,250 sq km (3,571 sq miles)
> POPULATION: 1,268,000
> CAPITAL CITY: Nicosia
> MAIN LANGUAGES: Greek, Turkish, English

Lebanon (Western Asia)

The green cedar tree has been a symbol of Lebanon for thousands of years – even the Ancient Egyptians bought cedar wood from the Lebanese. It represents immortality and steadfastness.

> AREA: 10,400 sq km (4,015 sq miles)
> POPULATION: 5,219,000
> CAPITAL CITY: Beirut
> MAIN LANGUAGES: Arabic, French, English

Syria (Western Asia)

This flag was partly inspired by the Pan-Arab flag (see right). The green stars represent Syria and Egypt, which formed a union called the United Arab Republic. The union ended in 1961, but Syria re-adopted the flag in 1980.
Similar: Egypt (29), Iraq (44).

> AREA: 185,180 sq km (71,498 sq miles)
> POPULATION: 24,348,000
> CAPITAL CITY: Damascus
> MAIN LANGUAGES: Arabic, Kurdish

Israel (Western Asia)

The emblem is the Shield of David, often called the Star of David, who was a king of ancient Israel. The star represents God, who protected him. The blue stripes echo the bands on the edges of traditional Jewish prayer shawls.

AREA: 20,770 sq km (8,019 sq miles)
POPULATION: 9,312,000
CAPITAL CITY: Jerusalem (disputed)
MAIN LANGUAGES: Hebrew, Arabic

Jordan (Western Asia)

Jordan's flag is based on the Pan-Arab flag described below. The star has seven points to represent *Al-Fatiha*, the seven-verse prayer that makes up the first chapter of the *Qur'an*, the holy book of Islam. Muslims recite it every day.

AREA: 89,342 sq km (34,495 sq miles)
POPULATION: 11,385,000
CAPITAL CITY: Amman
MAIN LANGUAGES: Arabic, English

The Pan-Arab flag

In 1916, Arab soldiers fighting in a desert revolt against the Ottoman Empire (see 28), raised a Pan-Arab flag which symbolized the identity of all Arabs. The flag represented important Muslim ruling families: black for the Abbasid Caliphs, who ruled from Baghdad; green for the Fatimid Caliphs of North Africa; and white for the Umayyad Caliphs of Damascus. The red triangle stands for the Hashemite clan, who ruled Mecca, the birthplace of the prophet Muhammad.

The Pan-Arab flag has inspired the flags of many Arab states, including Egypt (29), Sudan (29), Syria, Jordan, Kuwait (44), the United Arab Emirates (45) and Yemen (46).

Iraq (Western Asia)

The Arabic lettering in the middle means *God is the Greatest.* Arabic writing is read from right to left, so unlike most flags, this one is hoisted with the right-hand edge closest to the flagpole. **Similar:** Egypt (29), Syria (42)

AREA: 437,072 sq km (168,754 sq miles)
POPULATION: 46,524,000
CAPITAL CITY: Baghdad
MAIN LANGUAGES: Arabic, Kurdish

Kuwait (Western Asia)

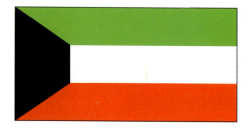

This flag's white, black, green and red each have their own meaning, described in this Kuwaiti poem: *White are our deeds, Black are our battles, Green are our lands, Red are our swords.*
Similar: UAE, Jordan (43)

AREA: 17,820 sq km (6,880 sq miles)
POPULATION: 4,349,000
CAPITAL CITY: Kuwait City
MAIN LANGUAGES: Arabic, English

Saudi Arabia (Western Asia)

The Arabic writing here reads *There is no god but God, and Muhammad is his messenger.* The sword symbolizes justice, and always points outward because, as with the flag of Iraq, the pole goes on the right.

AREA: 2,149,690 sq km (830,000 sq miles)
POPULATION: 37,474,000
CAPITAL CITY: Riyadh
MAIN LANGUAGES: Arabic

Bahrain (Western Asia)

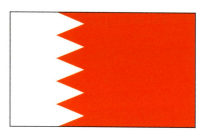

In 1933, the line dividing the red and white parts of this flag was changed from straight to jagged, to help distinguish the flag from many other local ones. The five white zigzag points represent the Five Pillars (duties) of Islam. **Similar:** Qatar

AREA: 741 sq km (286 sq miles)
POPULATION: 1,499,000
CAPITAL CITY: Manama
MAIN LANGUAGES: Arabic, English

Qatar (Western Asia)

The historic Qatari flag was bright red and white. According to legend, people noticed that the red dye darkened in the fierce sunlight and looked much more beautiful. So now all Qatari flags are maroon and white.

AREA: 11,437 sq km (4,416 sq miles)
POPULATION: 2,737,000
CAPITAL CITY: Doha
MAIN LANGUAGES: Arabic, English

UAE (Western Asia)

The flag of the **United Arab Emirates** is based on the Pan-Arab flag (see 43). Red echoes the flags of old Muslim states, green stands for the country's fertile land, white represents peace and black is for the oil deep underground. **Similar:** Kuwait

AREA: 83,600 sq km (32,278 sq miles)
POPULATION: 9,592,000
CAPITAL CITY: Abu Dhabi
MAIN LANGUAGES: Arabic, English

Flag proportions

As you look through this book you can see that, while the flags are shown at the same height, their width varies. Extreme examples are Switzerland (19), which is square, and Qatar, which with a ratio of 11:28 (that is, 11 units high and 28 units wide) is the widest flag. Most flags, like that of France (18), have a 2:3 ratio. The next most popular ratio is 1:2, for example, the Union Jack (15). These are ideal proportions, but cheaply-made flags are often all produced to the same ratio.

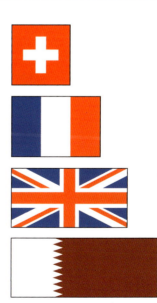

A range of flags, showing how flag proportions vary. From the top: Switzerland, France, the UK and Qatar

Yemen (Western Asia)

The flag was first flown in 1990, when North and South Yemen were unified. According to the official description, red stands for the bloodshed of martyrs, white for a bright future, and black for the dark past.
Similar: Egypt (29)

AREA: 527,970 sq km (203,850 sq miles)
POPULATION: 35,220,000
CAPITAL CITY: Sanaa
MAIN LANGUAGE: Arabic

Oman (Western Asia)

In the canton is Oman's national emblem. Two crossed swords lie beneath a *khanjar* – a curved ceremonial dagger. An ornate horsebit rests on top to show the Omani love of horses.

AREA: 309,500 sq km (119,499 sq miles)
POPULATION: 4,644,000
CAPITAL CITY: Muscat
MAIN LANGUAGES: Arabic, English, Baluchi

Georgia (Western Asia)

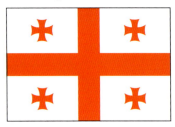

This flag has its roots in the Middle Ages. The large red cross is the banner of St George, Georgia's patron saint. The five crosses echo the Jerusalem Cross – a symbol carried by Christian soldiers fighting in religious wars known as the Crusades.

AREA: 69,700 sq km (26,911 sq miles)
POPULATION: 3,717,000
CAPITAL CITY: Tbilisi
MAIN LANGUAGES: Georgian, Russian

Armenia (Western Asia)

Mount Ararat, visible from Armenia's capital, is the nation's sacred symbol. This flag is said to have been inspired by the rainbow Noah saw over it, in the Bible story. Red stands for Armenia's highlands and its people's struggle. Blue speaks of a will to live under peaceful skies. Orange is for creativity and hard work.

AREA: 29,743 sq km (11,484 sq miles)
POPULATION: 2,778,000
CAPITAL CITY: Yerevan
MAIN LANGUAGE: Armenian

Azerbaijan (Western Asia)

The bands represent three important aspects of Azerbaijani culture. Blue stands for the people of Western Asia; red represents their everyday life, and green is for their religious life. The crescent and star symbolize Islam, the nation's main religion (see 28).

AREA: 86,600 sq km (33,436 sq miles)
POPULATION: 10,463,000
CAPITAL CITY: Baku
MAIN LANGUAGE: Azeri

Iran (Western Asia)

Iran's emblem represents *Allah* (God), and is also shaped like a tulip, a symbol of martyrdom (dying for your faith). Its five parts represent the Five Pillars (duties) of Islam. The square patterns are actually Arabic words, *Allahu Akbar*, which mean *God is the Greatest*, written 22 times.

AREA: 1,648,000 sq km (636,296 sq miles)
POPULATION: 89,810,000
CAPITAL CITY: Tehran
MAIN LANGUAGES: Farsi and other Persian dialects, Azeri

Kazakhstan (Central Asia)

Look closely and you'll see that the emblem shows a golden eagle flying beneath the sun. It represents the fierce independence of the Kazakhstani people. On the left is a traditional pattern called *koshkar-muiz*, which means *rams' horns*.

AREA: 2,717,300 sq km (1,049,155 sq miles)
POPULATION: 19,828,000
CAPITAL CITY: Astana
MAIN LANGUAGES: Kazakh, Russian

Turkmenistan (Central Asia)

The five designs on the band are called *guls*, traditionally woven into Turkmen carpets. They are the symbols of the country's five major tribes. The laurel wreath below is for neutrality. The stars and crescent symbolize Islam.

AREA: 488,100 sq km (188,456 sq miles)
POPULATION: 6,598,000
CAPITAL CITY: Ashgabat (Ashkhabad)
MAIN LANGUAGES: Turkmen, Russian

Uzbekistan (Central Asia)

A 14th-century conquerer named Tamerlane was born in Uzbekistan, and his standard was blue. The twelve stars represent the twelve regions of Uzbekistan, and the crescent stands for Islam, the country's main religion.

> **AREA:** 447,400 sq km (172,742 sq miles)
> **POPULATION:** 35,674,000
> **CAPITAL CITY:** Tashkent
> **MAIN LANGUAGES:** Uzbek, Russian

Kyrgyzstan (Central Asia)

Many Kyrgyz are nomads who spend their summers on the country's vast *steppes* (plains) in tents called *yurts*, to tend their flocks. Within the sun emblem is the round skylight of a yurt roof. The crossed curving lines are red-painted tent poles.

> **AREA:** 198,500 sq km (76,641 sq miles)
> **POPULATION:** 6,840,000
> **CAPITAL CITY:** Bishkek
> **MAIN LANGUAGES:** Kyrgyz, Russian, Uzbek

Tajikistan (Central Asia)

This flag shows a golden crown and seven stars – the number seven signifies perfection. Red is said to stand for the sun and victory; white for purity, cotton and snow on the mountains; and green for Islam and the riches of nature.
Similar: Hungary (25)

> **AREA:** 143,100 sq km (55,251 sq miles)
> **POPULATION:** 10,332,000
> **CAPITAL CITY:** Dushanbe
> **MAIN LANGUAGES:** Tajik, Russian

Afghanistan (Central–South Asia)

Afghanistan's emblem shows a mosque flanked by two flags. Below it, in Arabic, is written 1298, the date in the Islamic calendar when the country gained independence from the British Empire – 1919 in the Western calendar.

> **AREA:** 652,230 sq km (251,827 sq miles)
> **POPULATION:** 43,373,000
> **CAPITAL CITY:** Kabul
> **MAIN LANGUAGES:** Dari, Pashto

Pakistan (South Asia)

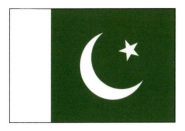

In Islam, green symbolizes life and prosperity. The green part of the flag represents Pakistan's Muslim majority; the white band, the smaller number who follow other religions. The star stands for the light of knowledge, and the crescent for progress.

AREA: 803,940 sq km (310,403 sq miles)
POPULATION: 245,210,000
CAPITAL CITY: Islamabad
MAIN LANGUAGES: Urdu, English, Punjabi, Pashto, Sindhi, Saraiki

India (South Asia)

The wheel in the middle is called the *Ashoka Chakra*. It symbolizes the teachings of the Buddhist faith, each of the 24 spokes representing a different virtue. All Indian flags are hand woven on a spinning wheel called a *charkha*.

AREA: 3,287,590 sq km (1,269,345 sq miles)
POPULATION: 1,441,720,000
CAPITAL CITY: New Delhi
MAIN LANGUAGES: Hindi, English, Bengali, Marathi, Telugu, Tamil, Urdu

Maldives (South Asia)

The earliest flag of the Maldives was plain red. The green rectangle with the white crescent was added later to represent the country's Islamic tradition (see 28). This flag was first flown in 1965.

AREA: 300 sq km (116 sq miles)
POPULATION: 518,000
CAPITAL CITY: Male
MAIN LANGUAGES: Maldivian, English

Sri Lanka (South Asia)

The four fig leaves around the Sri Lankan lion stand for Buddhism. Its founder, the Buddha, is said to have been sitting under a fig tree when he was *enlightened* – reaching a state of perfect understanding and bliss. The orange stripe represents the island's Tamil people, and the green its Muslims.

AREA: 65,610 sq km (25,332 sq miles)
POPULATION: 21,949,000
CAPITAL CITIES: Colombo, Sri Jayewardenepura Kotte
MAIN LANGUAGES: Sinhala, Tamil, English

Nepal (South Asia)

This, the world's only non-rectangular flag, combines the pennants of two old ruling families. Crimson symbolizes bravery and also the rhododendron, Nepal's national flower.

Crimson and deep blue are both popular in Nepali art. The sun and moon symbols also express a hope that Nepal will last as long as the heavenly bodies.

AREA: 147,181 sq km (56,827 sq miles)
POPULATION: 31,240,000
CAPITAL CITY: Kathmandu
MAIN LANGUAGES: Nepali, Maithili

Bhutan (South Asia)

The dragon is a symbol of Bhutan. The local name of this mountainous country means *Land of the Thunder Dragon*. The old flag was square, but people noticed it didn't flap in the breeze, so they made the new one rectangular.

AREA: 47,000 sq km (18,147 sq miles)
POPULATION: 792,000
CAPITAL CITY: Thimphu
MAIN LANGUAGES: Dzongkha, Nepali

The odd one out

It wasn't until the 18th century that European countries standardized their national flags. Rectangles turned out to be a handy shape, and nations around the world slowly adapted their own flags to match. For example, in 1897 Ethiopia (36) turned its traditional pennants into a modern rectangular flag. Remote **Nepal** was less affected by these trends, and even today, although a few Nepalese want a rectangular flag, most are proud to be different.

Ethiopia's pennants

Ethiopia's flag 1897–1974

50

Bangladesh (South Asia)

The red circle represents the rising sun, and it is a symbol of new hope after the country's long struggle for independence. The sun is positioned slightly nearer to the hoist edge, so that when the flag is fluttering it appears to be in the middle.

AREA: 144,000 sq km (55,599 sq miles)
POPULATION: 174,701,000
CAPITAL CITY: Dhaka
MAIN LANGUAGES: Bengali, English

Mongolia (East Asia)

The golden emblem on this flag is called the *Soyombo*. It represents various ideas. For example, the sun circle and crescent moon are symbols of the eternal Mongolian people. The tall rectangles represent a fortress and the idea that Mongolia's strength comes from its people's unity.

AREA: 1,564,116 sq km (603,909 sq miles)
POPULATION: 3,494,000
CAPITAL CITY: Ulan Bator
MAIN LANGUAGE: Mongolian

North Korea (East Asia)

This became the official flag when North Korea became an independent state in 1948. The red star symbolizes the country's communist beliefs (see 52). The combination of red, white and blue on flags is traditional in Korean culture.

AREA: 120,540 sq km (46,541 sq miles)
POPULATION: 26,245,000
CAPITAL CITY: Pyongyang
MAIN LANGUAGE: Korean

South Korea (East Asia)

The round symbol is called *Taeguk* in Korean. Like China's *yin-yang*, it depicts the belief that the world is made up of opposites that depend on each other. For example, it's hard to grasp what light is without an idea of darkness. The four signs stand for heaven, water, earth and fire.

AREA: 98,480 sq km (38,023 sq miles)
POPULATION: 51,742,000
CAPITAL CITY: Seoul
MAIN LANGUAGE: Korean

China (East Asia)

This flag was first flown in 1949, when the Communist* Party of China came to power. The large gold star is a symbol of China's Communist Party. The smaller stars stand for the four social classes that came together in unity.

AREA: 9,600,000 sq km (3,700,000 sq miles)
POPULATION: 1,425,179,000
CAPITAL CITY: Beijing
MAIN LANGUAGE: Mandarin Chinese

Hong Kong SAR** (East Asia)

Hong Kong was under Britain's colonial rule from 1841 until 1997, when it was returned to China. Its flag, like China's, is red with five stars. The white emblem is the flower of the Hong Kong orchid tree, symbolizing the port city's promised freedom to run its own affairs.

AREA: 1,114 sq km (430 sq miles)
POPULATION: 7,503,100
MAIN LANGUAGES: Cantonese, English

**Special Administrative Region

The red flag of communism

Over the course of history, red flags have become a symbol of revolution, flown for example at the 1848 Revolution in Paris, when French workers overthrew the king. In October 1917, the communist Bolshevik Party of Russia (27) defeated the government, and in 1922 founded the Soviet Union. Their new flag was red, for revolution, with a red star, representing communism, and a hammer and sickle, standing for factory and farm workers united in a common cause.

The red flag of the Soviet Union (1922–1991) influenced the flags of the communist countries China, North Korea (51) and Vietnam (54).

*Communism is a political system whose ultimate goal is that everyone shares equally in the wealth society produces, and that the government owns everything needed to create that wealth, on behalf of the people.

Macau SAR (East Asia)

Once under Portugal's colonial rule, Macau was returned to China in 1999, and still blends Chinese and Portuguese culture today. Along with the five stars of China, its flag bears a white lotus. Its three petals stand for Macau's peninsula and its islands, Taipa and Coloane.

> **AREA:** 33.3 sq km (12.9 sq miles)
> **POPULATION:** 704,000
> **MAIN LANGUAGES:** Cantonese, Portuguese

Japan (East Asia)

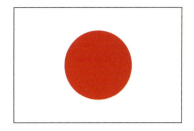

This flag is known as the *Hinomaru*. This means *Circle of the Sun* and it echoes Japan's local name, *Nihon*, which means *Land of the Rising Sun*. The flag has been in use since the 14th century but was made official in 1854.

> **AREA:** 377,835 sq km (145,883 sq miles)
> **POPULATION:** 122,631,000
> **CAPITAL CITY:** Tokyo
> **MAIN LANGUAGE:** Japanese

Myanmar (Southeast Asia)

The yellow, green and red stripes come from a flag that Myanmar, then known as **Burma**, flew in the 1940s. They are now said to stand for team spirit, peace and courage. The white star stands for purity, honesty, compassion and power.

> **AREA:** 678,500 sq km (261,970 sq miles)
> **POPULATION:** 54,965,000
> **CAPITAL CITIES:** Naypyidaw, Yangon (Rangoon)
> **MAIN LANGUAGE:** Burmese

Laos (Southeast Asia)

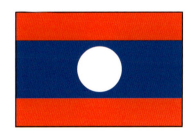

Laos is one of the few communist countries that doesn't have a star on its flag. The white circle on the blue band is said to echo a full moon shining on the Mekong River. Red symbolizes the blood that was shed as the country fought for its freedom.

> **AREA:** 236,800 sq km (91,429 sq miles)
> **POPULATION:** 7,737,000
> **CAPITAL CITY:** Vientiane
> **MAIN LANGUAGES:** Lao, French, English

Thailand (Southeast Asia)

The old Thai flag showed a white elephant* on red. When the king saw it flying upside down, he was so shocked he chose a new design to stop it happening again. Red, white and blue were inspired by the flags of Thailand's First World War allies. **Similar:** Costa Rica (7)

> **AREA:** 514,000 sq km (198,457 sq miles)
> **POPULATION:** 71,886,000
> **CAPITAL CITY:** Bangkok
> **MAIN LANGUAGES:** Thai, English, Chaochow

*Still visible on the Thai naval flag (see 62)

Cambodia (Southeast Asia)

The emblem on this flag is a picture of the Angkor Wat temple. It's the only building in the world to be shown on a national flag. This flag is Cambodia's seventh since 1948, when it became independent.

> **AREA:** 181,040 sq km (69,900 sq miles)
> **POPULATION:** 17,122,000
> **CAPITAL CITY:** Phnom Penh
> **MAIN LANGUAGES:** Khmer, French

Vietnam (Southeast Asia)

The red background and five-pointed star echo other communist flag designs (see 52). Red represents revolution, and the points of the star symbolize the united Vietnamese people: farmers, workers, soldiers, thinkers and young people.

> **AREA:** 329,560 sq km (127,244 sq miles)
> **POPULATION:** 99,498,000
> **CAPITAL CITY:** Hanoi
> **MAIN LANGUAGES:** Vietnamese, French, English, Khmer, Chinese

Malaysia (Southeast Asia)

The crescent and star are emblems of Islam, and yellow symbolizes royalty. There are 14 points on the star and 14 stripes, which represent the member states of the Federation of Malaysia. The flag was first used in 1963. **Similar:** USA (4)

> **AREA:** 329,750 sq km (127,317 sq miles)
> **POPULATION:** 34,672,000
> **CAPITAL CITIES:** Kuala Lumpur, Putrajaya
> **MAIN LANGUAGES:** Malay, English, Chinese dialects, Tamil

Singapore (Southeast Asia)

This flag was first flown in 1959, when the city of Singapore, then a British colony, became a self-governing state within the Empire. Red stands for the unity of all races; white for national purity and virtue. The five stars stand for democracy, peace, progress, justice and equality. **Similar:** Indonesia (56)

AREA: 693 sq km (267 sq miles)
POPULATION: 6,053,000
MAIN LANGUAGES: Chinese, Malay, English, Tamil

Brunei (Southeast Asia)

The emblem is Brunei's national crest, which represents Islam. The open arms symbolize the government's promise to serve the needs of the people. The lettering is in Arabic, and its meaning is *Always render service with God's guidance.*

AREA: 5,770 sq km (2,228 sq miles)
POPULATION: 456,000
CAPITAL CITY: Bandar Seri Begawan
MAIN LANGUAGES: Malay, English, Chinese

Stripes on flags

Bold, eye-catching stripes have been used on flags since at least the Middle Ages. 17th-century Portuguese merchant ships used green and white stripes, which may have inspired the English to use red and white. Seen wherever the ships sailed, these flags may have inspired others, including the USA (4), Greece (23), Indonesia (56) and Malaysia (left). The last two were probably also influenced by the red-and-white striped flag of the Majapahit Empire, which ruled the seas of Southeast Asia from the 13th–16th century.

Portuguese merchant

English East India Company

French merchant

55

Philippines (Southeast Asia)

The sun's rays represent eight Philippine provinces that rebelled against Spanish occupation in 1896. It is the only flag to be flown upside down when the country is at war; other nations have separate war flags (see 62). **Similar:** Czechia (24)

AREA: 300,000 sq km (115,831 sq miles)
POPULATION: 119,116,000
CAPITAL CITY: Manila
MAIN LANGUAGES: Filipino, English, Cebuano, Ilocano

Indonesia (Southeast Asia)

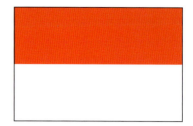

This flag symbolizes human life. Red stands for the body, and white represents the soul. The design is based on the flag of the 13th-century Majapahit Empire, which once included Indonesia. This flag is nearly identical to Poland's (24) – only its proportions differ.

AREA: 1,919,440 sq km (741,100 sq miles)
POPULATION: 279,798,000
CAPITAL CITY: Jakarta (a new capital, Nusantara, is being built)
MAIN LANGUAGES: Indonesian, Javanese, Sundanese, English, Dutch

East Timor (Southeast Asia)

This flag was first flown in 1975, but was banned after only nine days when Indonesia began its occupation of the country. The flag was readopted in 2002 when East Timor won its independence. The white star is a symbol of hope.

AREA: 15,007 sq km (5,794 sq miles)
POPULATION: 1,380,000
CAPITAL CITY: Dili
MAIN LANGUAGES: Tetum, Indonesian, Portuguese

Australia (Australasia)

Australia is part of the Commonwealth of Nations (see right), and has the Union Jack (15) on its flag. There's also a seven-pointed star on the left to symbolize Australia's states and territories. The stars on the right show the Southern Cross constellation.

AREA: 7,741,220 sq km (2,967,909 sq miles)
POPULATION: 26,699,000
CAPITAL CITY: Canberra
MAIN LANGUAGE: English

Norfolk Island (Australasia)

Norfolk Island is a tiny Australian territory lying between New Zealand and the French territory of New Caledonia. The emblem is the Norfolk Island pine, which grows only there. These towering trees were an ominous sight for arriving captives back when it was a prison island.

AREA: 35 sq km (13 sq miles)
POPULATION: 2,000
CAPITAL: Kingston
MAIN LANGUAGES: English, Norfuk

New Zealand (Australasia)

Like Australia, New Zealand's flag shows it was once a British colony. It also includes the four main stars of the Southern Cross constellation. They weren't made red for any particular reason, though native Maori people link red with the land and creation.

AREA: 268,680 sq km (103,738 sq miles)
POPULATION: 5,270,000
CAPITAL CITY: Wellington
MAIN LANGUAGES: English, Maori

The Commonwealth of Nations

The Commonwealth of Nations, "the Commonwealth" for short, was formed in 1931. It sees itself as a way for independent countries that mostly used to be British colonies to mark their historical connection. There are more than 50 Commonwealth realms, some of which still recognize the monarch of the United Kingdom (15) as their own head of state. They also aim to treat one other equally regardless of size or wealth, and to help each other.

This British Navy flag, the **Blue Ensign**, is the basis of a number of Commonwealth flags, including Australia (left), New Zealand (above), Fiji (58) and Tuvalu (60).

Papua New Guinea (Melanesia)

Papua New Guinea's flag was designed in a competition by 15-year-old student Susan Karike. Its emblems are the Southern Cross constellation and the raggiana bird-of-paradise, Papua New Guinea's national bird.

AREA: 462,840 sq km (178,704 sq miles)
POPULATION: 10,516,000
CAPITAL CITY: Port Moresby
MAIN LANGUAGES: Tok Pisin, Hiri Motu, English

Solomon Islands (Melanesia)

The Solomon Islands are made up of five groups of islands, represented by the stars. The blue triangle stands for the Pacific Ocean, and the green one for the islands' fertile land. The yellow stripe symbolizes the sun. This flag was first used in 1977.

AREA: 28,450 sq km (10,985 sq miles)
POPULATION: 757,000
CAPITAL CITY: Honiara
MAIN LANGUAGES: Pijin, English, Kwara'ae

Vanuatu (Melanesia)

The horizontal yellow "Y" shape represents the pattern in which the 83 islands of Vanuatu lie. The yellow swirl is a boar's tusk, a traditional Vanuatuan symbol of prosperity. The two fern fronds inside it symbolize peace.

AREA: 12,200 sq km (4,710 sq miles)
POPULATION: 342,000
CAPITAL CITY: Port Vila
MAIN LANGUAGES: Bislama, French, English

Fiji (Melanesia)

The Union Jack (15) and the lion at the top of the shield symbolize Fiji's historical links with Britain. The lion is not holding a rugby ball but a cacao pod – although rugby is Fiji's top sport! Fiji's coat of arms also pictures some of its main crops: sugar cane, coconuts and bananas, as well as a dove of peace.

AREA: 18,270 sq km (7,054 sq miles)
POPULATION: 943,000
CAPITAL CITY: Suva
MAIN LANGUAGES: Fijian, Hindi, English

Nauru (Micronesia)

Tiny Nauru is the smallest island nation. The 12-pointed star on its flag stands for its 12 original tribes. It lies just below the yellow line to reflect the country's position on a map. It is one degree south of the Equator, an imaginary line around the Earth.

AREA: 21 sq km (8 sq miles)
POPULATION: 13,000
CAPITAL: Yaren
MAIN LANGUAGES: Nauruan, English

Palau (Micronesia)

The yellow circle is a full moon, a symbol of national unity. In Palauan tradition, a full moon is seen as the best time for community activities such as fishing, harvesting, planting and festivals. The blue background represents the vast Pacific Ocean.

AREA: 458 sq km (177 sq miles)
POPULATION: 18,000
CAPITAL: Ngerulmud
MAIN LANGUAGES: Palauan, English, Filipino

Guam (Micronesia)

The largest of the Mariana Islands, Guam has been run by the USA since 1898, and is its westernmost territory. The emblem on its flag shows a view of Agaña Bay with a coconut palm and a *proas*, a type of boat used by the local Chamorro people.

AREA: 540 sq km (210 sq miles)
POPULATION: 173,000
CAPITAL: Hagåtña
MAIN LANGUAGES: Chamorro, English

FS Micronesia (Micronesia)

The **Federated States of Micronesia** is made up of over 600 islands. These are divided into four states, Yap, Chuuk, Kosrae and Pohnpei, which are represented by stars. This flag was inspired by the flag of the United Nations (see 63).

AREA: 702 sq km (271 sq miles)
POPULATION: 116,000
CAPITAL: Palikir
MAIN LANGUAGES: English, Chuukese, Pohnpeian

Marshall Islands (Micronesia)

The stripes represent the nation's two island chains. The western chain, Ralik, is shown in orange because its name means "sunset". The eastern chain, Ratak ("sunrise") is shown in white. The orange also stands for bravery and the white for peace. The star has 24 rays – one for each district.

> **AREA:** 181 sq km (70 sq miles)
> **POPULATION:** 42,000
> **CAPITAL CITY:** Majuro
> **MAIN LANGUAGES:** Marshallese, English

Kiribati (Micronesia)

This scenic flag shows a frigate bird soaring over the Pacific at sunrise. Each of the sun's rays represents one of the islands of Kiribati. The bird symbolizes power and freedom. This 1979 flag is based on the coat of arms of the Gilbert Islands from when it was a British colony.

> **AREA:** 811 sq km (313 sq miles)
> **POPULATION:** 136,000
> **CAPITAL:** South Tarawa
> **MAIN LANGUAGES:** Gilbertese, English

Tonga (Polynesia)

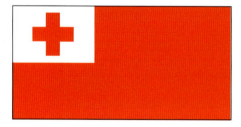

The cross is a symbol of Christianity. White stands for purity, and red for the blood shed by Jesus Christ when he was crucified. The original flag was white with a red cross, but it was too similar to the flag of the Red Cross (see 63). This design was chosen in 1875.

> **AREA:** 748 sq km (289 sq miles)
> **POPULATION:** 108,000
> **CAPITAL CITY:** Nuku'alofa
> **MAIN LANGUAGES:** Tongan, English

Tuvalu (Polynesia)

The yellow stars represent the nine islands of Tuvalu, and are arranged to show how they lie on a map. The Union Jack (15) in the corner is a symbol of the country's links with Britain and other members of the Commonwealth (see 57).

> **AREA:** 26 sq km (10 sq miles)
> **POPULATION:** 11,000
> **CAPITAL:** Funafuti
> **MAIN LANGUAGES:** Tuvaluan, English

Samoa (Polynesia)

The red on this flag is said to stand for courage, the blue for freedom, and the white for purity. Samoa used to be a territory of New Zealand (57) and shows this link with the Southern Cross constellation in the canton.

AREA: 2,944 sq km (1,137 sq miles)
POPULATION: 226,000
CAPITAL CITY: Apia
MAIN LANGUAGES: Samoan, English

American Samoa (Polynesia)

American Samoa is the southernmost territory of the USA. Its flag shows an American bald eagle carrying a Samoan war club and fly whisk. These symbolize the power of the state and Samoa's traditional chiefs.

AREA: 200 sq km (77 sq miles)
POPULATION: 44,000
CAPITAL: Pago Pago
MAIN LANGUAGES: Samoan, English

Cook Islands (Polynesia)

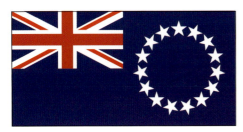

The Cook Islands is a small, self-governing nation associated with New Zealand, which helps defend it. Like New Zealand, it is a former British colony with a flag based on the Blue Ensign (see 57), plus a circle of stars representing its 15 islands.

AREA: 237 sq km (92 sq miles)
POPULATION: 17,000
CAPITAL: Avarua
MAIN LANGUAGES: English, Cook Islands Maori, Pukapukan

French Polynesia (Polynesia)

This territory of France is its only official overseas country. Its 121 islands cover a stretch of the South Pacific five times France's size. The largest island is Tahiti. The flag, flown alongside the French *Tricolore*, shows a traditional canoe on a background of sun and sea.

AREA: 4,167 sq km (1,609 sq miles)
POPULATION: 309,000
CAPITAL CITY: Pape'ete, Tahiti
MAIN LANGUAGES: French, Tahitian

Government flags

Some countries have special flags that only the government is allowed to fly. These are often variations of the national flag, for example with a coat of arms added or removed. A few examples are shown below. Nordic countries (see pages 16–17) often have government flags with a swallowtail shape.

Peru

Germany

Lithuania

Iceland

War flags and ensigns

The battle banners of fighting forces were some of the earliest versions of flags. They were often elaborate and impressive – flags glorious enough to die under. Some countries still have **war flags** today, used by ground forces. Flags used by navies at sea are called **naval ensigns**. These are large flags flown from the stern (rear) of warships to identify their nationality. They are often just the national flag or a variation with the national flag in the canton, but some more unusual examples are shown below. **Civil ensigns** (often red) are flown on merchant ships.

Other flags

Apart from national flags, international organizations, religions, peoples, regions and interest groups often fly flags of their own. How many have you spotted?

The European Union (EU) is a group of European nations that co-operate to promote peace, liberty and trade. The 12 gold stars on its flag stand for completeness, like 12 hours on a clock. The circle denotes unity.

The Olympic Games, held every four years, is the world's biggest multi-sport event. Its flag features five interlinked rings symbolizing the union of the five inhabited continents, whose many athletes join together to compete.

The United Nations (UN) works for peace, justice, progress and human rights. Nearly every independent country in the world is a member. The world map on its flag focuses on the North Pole so that no country has central place. The sky blue and olive branches symbolize peace.

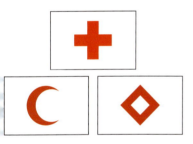

The **red cross**, **red crescent** and **red crystal** are international symbols of protection in war zones. They are also used by the **International Red Cross and Red Crescent Movement**, which works independently, not taking sides, to bring aid to all based on need alone.

The Buddhist flag was introduced in 1885 as an international symbol of the faith. Blue stands for compassion; yellow, the Buddhist Middle Way between extremes; red, blessing; white, purity; and saffron, wisdom.

The **Nishan Sahib** is the flag of the Sikh religion, often seen flying outside places of worship (*gurdwaras*). Upon the saffron pennant is the *Khanda*, the symbol of Sikhism, which represents truth, unity, eternity, and the need to defend faith.

The Australian Aboriginal flag is an official symbol of Australia (56). Black stands for the native Aboriginal peoples, the circle is for the Sun, and red is for the earth and for the red clay pigment used in sacred ceremonies.

Bougainville is a self-governing region of Papua New Guinea (58) that may become an independent country by the late 2020s. Regional flags are often used by independence movements.

The World Scout flag is flown at Scout gatherings worldwide. Its symbol, the fleur-de-lis, used to point north on old maps. It symbolizes that a Scout shows the way by doing their duty and helping others.

Index

Aboriginal flag 63
Afghanistan 48
Albania 24, 62
Algeria 28
Andorra 21
Angola 40
Antigua and Barbuda 10
Argentina 14
Armenia 46
Aruba 11
Australia 56, 63
Austria 20
Azerbaijan 47, 62
Bahamas 7
Bahrain 44
Bangladesh 51
Barbados 11
Belarus 26
Belgium 18, 62
Belize 5
Benin 33
Bermuda 5
Bhutan 50
Blue Ensign 57
Bolivia 13
Bosnia and Herzegovina 23
Botswana 41
Bougainville 63
Brazil 13
Brunei 55
Buddhism 63
Bulgaria 27
Burkina Faso 32
Burma (see Myanmar, 53)
Burundi 38
Cambodia 54
Cameroon 34
Canada 4
Cape Verde 30
Cayman Islands 8
Central African Republic 35
Chad 34
Chile 14
China 52, 62
Colombia 12
Comoros 38
Congo, Republic of the 35
Congo, Democratic
   Republic of the 35
Cook Islands 61
Costa Rica 7
Côte d'Ivoire (see
   Ivory Coast, 32)
Croatia 22
Cuba 7
Cyprus 42
Czechia 24
Denmark 17
Djibouti 36
Dominica 10
Dominican Republic 8
East Timor 56
Ecuador 13
Egypt 29
El Salvador 6
Equatorial Guinea 34
Eritrea 36
Estonia 17, 62
Eswatini 41
Ethiopia 36, 50
European Union 63
Faroe Islands 16
Fiji 58
Finland 17
France 18
French Polynesia 61
Gabon 35
Gambia, The 30
Georgia 46
Germany 19
Ghana 32
Greece 23
Greenland 5
Grenada 11
Guam 59
Guatemala 6
Guinea 31
Guinea-Bissau 31
Guyana 12
Haiti 8
Honduras 6
Hong Kong SAR 52
Hungary 25
Iceland 16
India 49
Indonesia 56
Iran 47
Iraq 44
Ireland 15
Israel 43
Italy 21
Ivory Coast 32
Jamaica 8
Japan 53, 62
Jordan 43
Kazakhstan 47
Kenya 37
Kiribati 60
Korea, North 51
Korea, South 51
Kosovo 24
Kuwait 44
Kyrgyzstan 48
Laos 53
Latvia 17
Lebanon 42
Lesotho 41
Liberia 31
Libya 29
Liechtenstein 20
Lithuania 18
Luxembourg 18
Macedonia, North 23
Macau SAR 53
Madagascar 39
Malawi 39
Malaysia 54
Maldives 49
Mali 32
Malta 22, 62
Marshall Islands 60
Mauritania 30
Mauritius 39
Mexico 5
Micronesia, Federated
   States of 59
Moldova 26
Monaco 19
Mongolia 51
Montenegro 23
Morocco 29
Mozambique 39
Myanmar (Burma) 53
Namibia 40
Nauru 59
Nepal 50
Netherlands 19
New Zealand 57
Nicaragua 6
Niger 33
Nigeria 33
Norfolk Island 57
Norway 16
Olympic Games 63
Oman 46
Ottoman Empire 28
Pakistan 49, 62
Palau 59
Panama 7
Papua New Guinea 58, 63
Paraguay 14
Peru 13, 62
Philippines 56
Poland 24
Portugal 20
Puerto Rico 9
Qatar 45
Red Crescent 63
Red Cross 63
Red Crystal 63
Romania 26
Russia 27, 62
Rwanda 37
St Kitts and Nevis 9
St Lucia 10
St Vincent and the
   Grenadines 10
Samoa 61
Samoa, American 61
San Marino 21
Sao Tome and Principe 34
Saudi Arabia 44
Scout Movement 63
Senegal 30
Serbia 22
Seychelles 38
Sierra Leone 31
Sikhism 63
Singapore 55, 62
Slovakia 25
Slovenia 22
Solomon Islands 58
Somalia 37
South Africa 41
South Sudan 36
Soviet Union 52
Spain 20
Sri Lanka 49
Sudan 29
Suriname 12
Swaziland (see Eswatini, 41)
Sweden 16
Switzerland 19
Syria 42
Tajikistan 48
Tanzania 38
Thailand 54, 62
Timor-Leste (see East Timor, 56)
Togo 33
Tonga 60
Trinidad and Tobago 11
Tunisia 28
Turkey 42
Turkmenistan 47
Tuvalu 60
Uganda 37
Ukraine 26
United Arab Emirates 45
United Kingdom 15, 62
United Nations 63
Uruguay 14
United States of America 4
Uzbekistan 48
Vanuatu 58
Vatican City State 21
Venezuela 12
Vietnam 54
Virgin Islands, British 9
Virgin Islands, United States 9
Yemen 46
Yugoslavia (see Pan-Slavic flag, 27)
Zambia 40
Zimbabwe 40

List of features

Commonwealth of Nations, The	57
Flag proportions	45
Flags and heraldry	25
Government flags	62
Odd one out, The (Nepal)	50
Pan-African flags (see Ghana)	32
Pan-Arab flag, The	43
Pan-Slavic flag, The	27
Red flag of communism, The	52
Star and crescent, The	28
Stars and stripes, History of the	4
Stripes on flags	55
United Kingdom, Flags of the	15
War flags and naval ensigns	62

Credits

Flag illustrations courtesy of The Flag Institute
Additional flag illustrations by Keith Furnival
With thanks to Jos Poels and Ruth Brocklehurst
Flags on p63 used by by kind permission of: The European Union; The International Committee of the Red Cross; The International Olympic Committee; The United Nations; The World Organization of the Scout Movement.

First published in 2024 by Usborne Publishing Limited, 83–85 Saffron Hill, London ECIN 8RT, United Kingdom. **usborne.com** Copyright © 2024 Usborne Publishing Limited. The name Usborne and the Balloon logo are registered trade marks of Usborne Publishing Limited. All rights reserved. No part of this publication may be reproduced, stored in a retrieval system, or transmitted in any form or by any means without prior permission of the publisher. First published in America 2025. UE.